Mother Knows Best

by
Karen Javitch
and
Amy Friedman

Illustrated by
Frances Thurber Kreuz

© Karen Javitch & Amy Friedman, 1982

LIBERTY PUBLISHING COMPANY
Cockeysville, Maryland

Published by:
Liberty Publishing Company, Inc.
50 Scott Adam Road
Cockeysville, Maryland 21030

Library of Congress # 81-85000
ISBN 0-89709-032-2

Manufactured in USA

To our husbands,
Gary and Sandy,
for their love, support and help
and
to our children
Jennifer & Mark
Andrea & Dustin
for being our inspirations!

Mother Knows Best is an exciting new book that deals with child care from the mother's perspective rather than the sheltered perspective of the physician's office. Its helpful hints on how to supervise your child's problems during the first four years of life will indeed be a revelation to many mothers. The sharing of experience which is offered in this book shows a very pragmatic and easy way to overcome many of the rough spots of early motherhood.

I wholeheartedly endorse this book and recommend it to all mothers caring for children aged four and younger.

Philip G. Itkin, M.D., F.A.A.P.

Contents

Daily Care   **3**
...sleeping habits...bathing...diapers

Feeding Time   **35**
...nursing...bottle-feeding...feeding toddlers...self-feeding...clean-up...a nourishing diet...fussy eaters

Household Organization???   **59**
...organizing...making dinner...organizing clothes...decorating Baby's room

On The Move   **73**
...trip preparation... air travel...car travel... shopping...visiting in-town...dining out

Avoiding Accidents   **89**
...inside and outside the house...safety hints... first aid help

Illness   **111**
...doctor visits...a sick child

More Than One   **129**
...preparing...Mommy in the hospital...Baby's arrival...jealousy...twins

Growing Up   **149**
...crib to bed...toilet training...shoes... little helpers...learning new things

Miscellaneous   **165**
...finding time for yourself...baby sitters... time & money-saving ideas...pets...playtime ...birthday parties...recommended reading

Acknowledgements   **191**

Index   **193**

Preface

Every mother will admit to a few disasters during her on-the-job training. If possible, it is better to learn from the experiences of *others* rather than from your own mistakes. In fact, this is the purpose of this book. We asked mothers from across the country to give us their hints on raising children from infancy through four years of age. Included are ideas chosen from more than 1,000 suggestions to make motherhood an easier, more enjoyable job. These "veterans" of our trade have discovered what to do if Baby decides morning starts at 4:00 A.M., or how to amuse a toddler throughout a long and dreary winter. And they know a few ways to save money on expensive children's items.

To give each mom the recognition she deserves, we put her name and hometown following her hint(s). In this text, the term "Authors" refers to either or both of us, or to Francie, our illustrator. Should any fathers feel left out of the book, it was certainly not our intent. It just happened that only women sent us hints on childrearing. We would like to stress, however, that the information in this book would also apply to dads or anyone involved in child care.

Of course, the hints reflect many different philosophies on childrearing. It's up to the reader to decide which hints best suit the situation or the needs of the child. Some may not work now, but could succeed at a later time. Some ideas may seem obvious, but are included because each of us occasionally overlooks the easy answer. Other hints will strike you as brilliant! We have simply gathered many useful "secrets" to help at the business of mothering.

We think *Mother Knows Best* will help you avoid some of the perils along your journey through Motherhood. It's a trip sure to take you through the best times of your life and perhaps a few of the worst! So read on, because in Motherhood there is no turning back. No exits and no U-turns are allowed!

Karen & Amy

Daily Care

Sleeping: Newborns....................6

Sleeping: Babies Three
    Months and Up....................10

Sleeping: One to
    Four Years Old....................16

Bathing: Babies....................19

Bathing: One to
    Four Years Old....................23

Diapering...........................26

A VISIT TO SLUMBERLAND

It is important for Baby to develop good sleeping habits and it doesn't hurt Mom either! The first time your infant sleeps through the night, you may jerk awake and run to the crib to make sure Shnookums is still breathing. Such anxiety probably won't last long and soon you will come to depend on an eight hour span of uninterrupted slumber. Even six hours can be a blessing.

Amazing things happen once you rediscover peaceful sleep. The fog will clear out of your brain. For the first time in months you will see in focus. Bet you never realized Shnookums had such a loveable grin. Your husband begins to look sexy again. Congratulations! You have returned from the land of zombies. These hints will insure that you don't go back.

LAYETTE AND NURSERY NEEDS FOR SLEEPING BABY

Furniture

Crib
Bassinet or cradle*
Swinging portable crib*
Portable crib*

Bedding

1 waterproof mattress
3-5 receiving blankets
2 lightweight crib blankets
1 warm crib blanket
2-3 fitted crib sheets
6 small waterproof pads
2 rubber sheets to protect mattress
2 crib sheets for bassinet*
1 comforter or quilt*
crib bumper pad
crib mobile

*Items that are nice to have, but not necessary.

INFANT'S CLOTHING NEEDS
4-6 cotton shirts
3 gowns or sacque sets
3 pajama stretch suits (medium and large sizes)
3-5 receiving blankets
4 waterproof panties (if used)
booties or socks
1 sweater or bonnet
1 cap or bonnet
1 pram suit or bunting (depending on weather)
1 blanket sleeper for wintertime
dress-up outfits if desired for company or travel

Sleeping Hints: Newborns

FAVORITE COLOGNE

During those crazy, desperate, newborn days, try something to soothe both Mom and Baby. Wear a favorite cologne in the hospital! It'll lift your spirits and help Baby associate the fragrance with you. When you get home, continue using it and spray some on a soft crib toy. Put the toy near your newborn for comfort when she's in the crib and you can't be there.

Karen Maizel
Lakewood, Ohio

HEATING PAD

This hint really worked for me, especially in the first few weeks. While baby was being fed and diapered, I heated her crib by placing a heating pad on *low* in the bed. It made the bed warm and more like the temperature inside the womb. I then took the heating pad out of the bed, put the baby back in her crib and she fell right to sleep.

Betsy Johnston Brewer
Arlington, Texas

TIGHT BLANKET

Remember that newborns usually love to be swaddled. A good, tight, snuggly fit blanket can often soothe a cranky newborn.

Donna Hatfield
Monrovia, California

PEACEFUL SLUMBER

My baby slept through the night when she was six weeks old. I did three things: 1) At her 10:00 feeding, I nursed her until she was full, and then I changed her. 2) I turned on an "easy listening" FM station on a radio on a bureau next to her bed. 3) I wrapped her tightly in a receiving blanket in what I call the "hospital wrap" and laid her on her tummy. These three things worked like a charm until her 5:00 A.M. feeding. Those seven hours of uninterrupted sleep really did wonders for me!

Inez Davis
Kansas City, Missouri

HAIR DRYER

My baby was very colicky during his second month. I discovered that when I was blow-drying his hair (with the hand-held dryer on *low* setting), he would fall asleep. Evidently the combination of the warm air on his head plus the hum of the hair dryer did the trick!

Susan J. Blair
Omaha, Nebraska

A SOOTHING BATH

If your infant is mixing up his days and nights, a bath at night may help solve the problem. The warm water relaxes a baby and makes it easier for him to fall asleep.

Deborah Sawyer
Dracut, Massachusetts

AVERAGE SLEEP SCHEDULE

Newborn...............	Average newborn may sleep anywhere from 10½ to 23 hours a day. Can have 10 to 12 sleeping periods each day.
6 weeks to............ 3 months	Baby tends to go to sleep after a feeding. Sleeps about 16 hours a day, having more wake periods. May have one time where he sleeps 6 hours (hopefully, at night).
3 months to........... 6 months	Stays awake longer. Most babies will begin to sleep through the night. May take four naps a day, then three.
6 months of age........	Sleeps about 12 hours at night. May take two or three naps during the day. Longest nap is probably in the morning.
1 year-old.............	Needs about 14-16 hours of sleep. Takes one or two naps a day.
1½ year-old...........	Down to one nap a day.
2 year-old.............	Sleeps about 12 hours at night, with up to two hours of sleep at naptime.
3-to-4 year-old........	May sleep 12 hours at night. A 3-year-old usually naps, but it shortens as child grows older. A 4-year-old may refuse to nap, but still needs rest period.

NEWBORN TERMS

(List of terms with which you may not be familiar but could need to know:)

Apgar Score - A method of rating a newborn's health. Scale ranges from 1-10. A visual exam is performed at one minute and at five minutes after birth.

Circumcision - This operation cuts away the foreskin from the head of the penis.

Chafing - A skin problem caused by friction of clothing against the skin, or by body surfaces rubbing together. Plump babies have skin folds that are prone to this. Treatment is to keep areas dry and use plain talcum powder.

Colostrum - Yellow fluid contained in the milk glands before the true milk comes in. It has helpful antibodies for the newborn baby.

Episiotomy - Incision in the mother's perineum to prevent tearing of the tissues during delivery. Repaired by obstetrician as soon as the baby is born.

Fontanels - Soft spots on top of a baby's head. Areas where the bones of the skull have not yet grown together.

Forceps - Special surgical instruments used sometimes to deliver a baby.

Impetigo in Newborn - A contagious skin infection. Small blister leaves a tiny raw spot. Starts in a moist place on Baby's body. New spots can occur. TREATMENT: Contact your doctor. It will spread if not properly treated. If you cannot reach him, use a piece of cotton to carefully wipe off the blister (don't spread the pus). This will expose the raw spot to air. Boil Baby's laundry daily. Then wash and dry them in hot sun. Baby's spoons should be sterilized, as should his bathtub.

Jaundice - Causes the skin, whites of the eyes and mucous membrane to turn yellow. Present in many premature infants and in about one-half of all full-term babies. It shows up around the second or third day after birth and begins to disappear before the fifth day. Your doctor should be notified if it lasts more than a week.

Lanugo - Fine, downy hair on the newborn that sheds in a week or two.

Mongolian Spot - A bluish-gray spot found on the lower part of the back. Often found in dark skinned infants. The spot gradually disappears as the child gets older.

Postpartum Depression - Also called ''Childbirth Blues.'' A brief period of depression often following childbirth. Could be related to hormone changes or psychological changes.

Vernix - A white creamy substance that covers the skin of the newborn infant. It provided skin protection in the womb.

Sleeping Hints:
Babies Three Months and Up

AVOIDING 2:00 A.M. FEEDINGS

When my baby reached 3 months of age, she suddenly decided she'd like to start her 2:00 A.M.
feeding again. I solved the problem by mixing two
tablespoons of cereal with her formula for her last
feeding before bed. A full tummy helped her sleep
longer. After a few days, I started to reduce the
amount of cereal each night until it was just formula.
She has slept through the night ever since except
when she is sick.

> *Inez Davis*
> *Kansas City, Missouri*

RECEIVING BLANKET

I put a receiving blanket over the sheet in the crib.
It keeps the bed warmer for the baby, and if the baby
spits up or wets, the blanket can be removed and
washed without changing the sheet. This also works
by using a diaper.

> *Shirley Pitcher*
> *Omaha, Nebraska*

LETTING BABIES CRY

Is your baby having sleeping problems? This may sound cruel, but after babies are fed, changed, and cuddled, let them cry. Sometimes it takes up to one-half hour before they will fall asleep.

Mothers from New London
New London, New Hampshire

When my baby was 3 months old, she started crying when I put her in the crib. I would feed her, change her, and then rock her to sleep, but as soon as I placed her in the crib, she would wake up and cry. She just did not want to be left alone. Since I didn't want her to get spoiled, I did the hardest thing: I let her cry. I also left a radio playing soft music next to her bed and closed her door. Each successive night she cried less and less.

Inez Davis
Kansas City, Missouri

SOOTHING SOUND

When my baby was 3 months old and he was crying inconsolably, I would hold him and stand in front of the sink and I'd turn the water on full blast. It was very soothing for him to hear the sound of the water, and watching it diverted his attention and he'd stop crying.

Authors
Omaha, Nebraska

FLEXIBILITY

Regarding the baby who decides that morning starts at 4:30 A.M.: So what! It won't last for long. No schedule does. The minute mom finally realizes, for instance, that 11:30 A.M. is a perfect time for lunch, bingo! Baby stops sleeping in the morning and lunch has to be rescheduled. I knew that the only way to survive is to remain flexible! So, if Baby wants to start the day at the crack of dawn for a while, let him!

Barbara Arkin
Roselle, Illinois

EARLY WAKE-UP

If your little one decides to start the day with the birds, try to make the room darker. The light of dawn may be waking up the baby. If the nursery has light, frilly curtains or too many windows, try putting the baby in a portable crib in a room that has heavier curtains or less windows.

Authors
Omaha, Nebraska

About the time my daughter became 6 months old, she would automatically wake up each morning when she heard her daddy walking down the hall to go to work. Unfortunately, he left much earlier than I cared to get up. We solved the problem by running a humidifier in her room. The hum of the humidifier muffled the sound of daddy leaving, and she would sleep a few hours longer. Also, the extra humidity is good for babies, especially in the winter-time when the house is dry.

Authors
Omaha, Nebraska

IS YOUR CRIB SAFE?

* The distance between crib slats should not exceed 2 3/8 inches.

* The height of the crib side from the bottom of the mattress (at its lowest position) to the top part of the railing should be at least 26 inches. This will keep Baby from climbing out easily.

* Your crib needs a mattress that fits snugly. You should be able to get two fingers or less between the mattress and the sides of the crib.

* Bumper pads need to be tied or snapped onto the crib in *six or more* places.

* There should be no horizontal bars that could help Baby climb out.

* There should be no toys in the crib large enough for Baby to step on so she could climb out.

* Put the mattress on its lowest position when Baby starts standing.

SLEEPING SCHEDULE

Our pediatrician emphasized the importance of having baby on a good, rigid, schedule, even if he was visiting or travelling. All I can say is that it has worked for me! Our 17-month-old boy knows exactly when its nap and bedtime, and *never* makes a sound when he's put in the crib. You must start as soon as the baby is brought home, and you must be consistent. It even helps the child to feel secure. When you first try it, you might have to let the baby cry. But usually after just one night, they get the hint!

Jeannine Adams
Atlanta, Georgia

Putting the baby or toddler to bed for a nap at the same time each day helps his body know when it's time to sleep, and he knows what to expect. Sometimes he needs to be *made* to stop playing when it's bedtime, but he appreciates it when his head finally hits the pillow.

Helen Cain
Omaha, Nebraska

LEAVE THE NOISES

Don't bother to turn down the noises of the house during sleeping hours! It's important for a baby to learn to sleep through noises so a knock on the door or a dog's bark won't ruin a nap.

Sheri Van Oosten
Omaha, Nebraska

NAP TIME

It took me nearly a year to realize that it is actually *easier* to let my two children sleep for naps at different times (they're two years apart). This allows each one to have individual time alone with me.

Colleen Brady
Rockford, Illinois

TOYS IN THE CRIB

I always keep a few *small* toys or books in baby's crib to entertain him in the morning when he wakes up.

Linda Vogel
Omaha, Nebraska

To encourage Baby to play in the crib in the morning, I attached a strainer (one with handles on both sides) to the side of her crib, and filled it with small toys and cloth books. In the morning when she awakens and stands up, there's something to keep her busy for awhile.

Mari Calianno
Dracut, Massachusetts

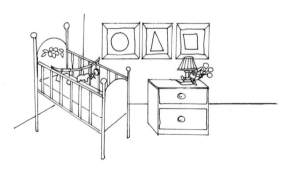

COMMON SLEEP PROBLEMS OF YOUNG CHILDREN

Problem and Age	Description	Possible Solutions
Colic: To 3 months	Colic occurs in roughly 10-15% of all babies and the cause is not really known. It usually comes at the same time each day (late afternoon or evening). The baby continuously cries as if he's in pain and has a tummy ache. His face becomes red and his abdomen is hard. He may pass gas. Colic occurs more often in firstborns.	Try these things: gentle comforting, quiet walking, or rocking in a rocking chair. Burp baby often while feeding. Try a pacifier, baby swing. Quietly talk or sing. Put Baby across your knees or on a warm hot-water bottle and rub his back. Let someone else (Dad, Grandma or a sitter) rock Baby for a while so Mom can have a break. DON'T overfeed Baby, supplement your breast milk, or get upset.
Post-Colic crier: 3 months and up	Child wakes up and cries in the middle-of-the night so he can be comforted. Many times it's a bad habit stemming from when the baby was colicky. Now he wants the comfort even though he is not colicky.	Go into the bedroom 5-10 minutes after the crying begins. Comfort Baby by rubbing his back while he's in his crib. Or try letting Baby cry. Baby will probably cry less and less with each successive night and usually by the 3rd night there's no more crying. DON'T move the crib into your bedroom.
Separation Anxiety: 6-12 months	Baby is starting to have separation anxiety and wakes suddenly in the night with a scream. He is fearful because Mom is not there. Possibly Baby is having his first dreams.	Gently and quietly comfort him. Speak softly with low lights. Pat his back. DON'T start feedings again.
1-2 year-old	Common for children this age to fuss before going to bed at night. May start to cry when Mom walks out of his room. Also common for child to wake up in the middle-of-the-night, sometimes crying in a loud, piercing cry (may be caused by bad dreams).	Many times his initial cry is a test, and he'll cry for only a few minutes and then go to sleep. If he awakens with a sudden, loud cry, go to him immediately and rub his back in his crib. During this time he may learn to climb out of his crib. Check often if this is so.
Separation Anxiety: 2 year-old	Child is probably feeling a little worried about staying alone in his room. He stalls by asking for a drink of water (even though he already had one), or saying he has to go potty (again). May also climb out of crib.	Be friendly but firm. Kiss and say good night and leave the room and don't look back. If child climbs out of crib, return to crib immediately to discourage making a game out of the activity.
Extreme Separation Anxiety: 2 year-old	Child is extremely afraid of going to bed. Can stay up for hours.	Sit by the crib or bed until the child has fallen asleep. Could possibly take weeks for the child to overcome the fear but it should work. During this time, DON'T go on any trips without the child. Possibly allow a sibling to sleep in 2 year-old's room for a while.
Night Wanderer: 3-5 years	Parents will find their child in their bedroom wanting to get into their bed with them.	DON'T be mad. Immediately and firmly return child back to his own bed.

Sleeping Hints:
One-to Four-Year-Olds

NOT IN THE DARK

I never put my children to bed at night or at nap time in a dark room. I always use a night light or leave the window shade partially up. They sleep well and are happy when they wake up.

Cheryl Foral
Omaha, Nebraska

LONG ROUTINE

A bedtime routine is nice, but not if it gets too lengthy for Mom and Dad. When my daughter was about two-years-old we got into this long "goodbye" routine to all of her dollies and stuffed animals. She then had to give them all "drinks." This took so long that I became very frustrated.

Authors
Omaha, Nebraska

SPECIAL PLAY AREA

If your toddler can't sleep, make a special closed-in area and let him play, but by himself. Let him know it is nighttime and you would rather he would be sleeping. Don't play with him, but if he just can't sleep, this does give him something to do.

Mothers from New London
New London, New Hampshire

GETTING RID OF MONSTERS

At bedtime my 3½ year-old daughter becomes very concerned with monsters. They may not be real to us, but they are very real to her. When she says there are monsters in her room, we all go through a big production. We yell at them to get out. By the time we've done, she is laughing. What could have been a disaster has turned into a comedy!

Mary Jane DiChiacchio
Landsdowne, Pennsylvania

TAPE SONGS AND STORIES

We make cassette tapes of my 2½-year-old's favorite songs and stories and play the tape on low volume to help him fall asleep at night.

Authors
Omaha, Nebraska

TALKING ABOUT THE DAY

When we put our toddler to sleep, we like to talk about what we did that day and what we're going to do tomorrow. This helps develop comprehension, communication, and self-esteem. It's more enjoyable to talk in the dark or with a night light on.

Helen Cain
Omaha, Nebraska

ADDED SECURITY

When I read a small book to my toddler before he is ready for bed, I finish by telling him I will see him in the morning. By doing this when I tuck him in at night it gives him the added assurance of knowing we won't be separated for long.

Susan Trotter
Rockford, Illinois

BEDTIME IS FUN

Never use bedtime as a threat. Simply announce that it will soon be time for sleep and as an added incentive, sing songs and wave good night to all of your child's dolls or stuffed animals. Make bedtime a fun ritual.

Mary Jane DiChiacchio
Lansdowne, Pennsylvania

ROCKING CHAIR

I recommend the use of a rocking chair, not only for a baby, but also for a toddler. It's the perfect way to help an active toddler unwind at the end of a day. The rocking chair has become a night-time ritual for me and my 2 year-old. The physical closeness is wonderful for both of us.

Authors
Omaha, Nebraska

BATH TIME - SCRUB A DUB DUB IT'S FUN IN THE TUB!

Few thrills equal the smell of a freshly washed baby. It takes the mother of a toddler to appreciate this. If your child has discovered the joys of gardening with indoor plants or massaging lunch into his scalp, you understand exactly what we mean. The excitement grows as you throw Little Piggie into the tub and watch the soapy bubbles dissolve the first layer of peanut butter and potting soil. You experience a rush of joy at the sight of shiny pink cheeks. Finally, the peak of ecstasy, you discover hair you can pull a comb through. Sounds great, doesn't it?

Unfortunately children don't always take to water. It's no fun for Baby or Mom to battle through bath time. These ideas will bring fun to the tub for both of you. Here's to smooth sailing!

Bathing Hints: Babies

HELP IN THE TUB

The sponge-like inserts for infants' tubs are great for a new baby and can be used in the regular tub, as the baby grows. They are inexpensive, washable, and they allow you to use both of your hands for washing the baby.

Rodeane Green
Glendale, Arizona

INFANT SEAT

The plastic infant seats are marvelous for the bath. Take the pad out, and put the baby and the infant seat in the sink or tub. Don't forget to strap him in. There is no chance of slipping or dropping the baby. He's comfortable and you feel at ease to enjoy bath time!

Mrs. Dawn Skinner
East Hartford, Connecticut

BATHING NEEDS
(Keep bath supplies handy in a basket or tray)

3-5 washcloths
2-3 bath towels (the hooded kind is good for Baby)
Portable baby bathtub (although a kitchen sink will do)
Small towel to put in bottom of tub so baby won't slide
Brush and comb
Mild soap for Baby's use only
Baby shampoo
Bath thermometer (not necessary although some parents feel more
    comfortable using it)
Nail scissors
Cotton swabs
Petroleum jelly
Ointment for diaper rash
Baby lotion, oil, powder or cornstarch

DID YOU KNOW that daily bathing is not recommended for infants as it may give them dry skin? Twice a week is usually adequate. Between baths, keep Baby's face and hands clean. Of course, Baby's bottom should be washed with water or wipes following each bowel movement.

BATHING AN INFANT

1. Room temperature should be 75-80 degrees in a room free of drafts.

2. Have all items necessary for bath together.

3. Never bathe a newborn in an adult bathtub. It is too hard to handle a baby when you are stooping over.

4. Test the water temperature with your elbow. You want it to be comfortably warm.

5. Keep Baby's head supported.

6. Wash the face first with a washcloth. Don't use soap.

7. Gently massage the scalp with soap, then do the rest of the body, saving the diaper area for last. Twice a week is plenty for washing the scalp.

8. Quietly talk to your baby, so he won't become frightened.

9. Pat rather than rub Baby dry. Be sure and dry creases of armpits and groin areas also.

10. NEVER LEAVE BABY ALONE IN TUB.

BABY TUB

After baby is too big to use his baby tub, don't store it away in your basement. There are many different ways to use it. My children have used it to store some favorite toys, sled with it in the winter, and they've filled it with water and played in it in the summertime.

Authors
Omaha, Nebraska

ANCHOR SEAT

One of the things that makes bath time more fun for the baby and parents is an Anchor Seat. It suctions to the tub and straps the baby in, which is especially helpful when baby's sitting isn't very stable.

Jeannine D. Adams
Atlanta, Georgia

LAUNDRY BASKET

Once your infant can sit up, you can begin giving him baths in the tub. Place a rectangular laundry basket in the bathtub and put your infant in that. He can hang onto the sides and this allows him to enjoy a bigger bath area while still feeling secure.

Mrs. Lee Goodspeed
Broadalbin, New York

DISHWASHER

When my son was a newborn, he seemed very frightened about being unswaddled for a bath. I solved the problem by giving him a sponge bath on top of the dishwasher while it was running. The vibration and warmth were very comforting to him.

Jan Peck
Goleta, California

AFTER BATH

My 3-month-old daughter is very active. She won't stay still long enough for me to dress her after her daily bath. I was very frustrated until I discovered that a small toy or rattle would divert her attention and keep her busy but still.

Now I always keep a toy near the changer or crib, where I can reach for it quickly. I introduce the toy with a little song, jingle, or game. She instantly becomes fascinated and plays contentedly. I change the toy every three or four days so that she won't become bored with it.

Debbie Sessions
Aiken, South Carolina

A BATH FOR TWO

It was hard for me to decide where to bathe my
10-month-old son. He was too big for his baby tub
and the kitchen sink, yet it was uncomfortable ben-
ding over to bathe him in the big tub. The best solution for me was to take a bath with him! It was comfortable, and he could play freely and safely!

Authors
Omaha, Nebraska

NO SLIPPING

A diaper or towel draped over the side and down
into the baby's bathtub is a real help. It keeps the
baby from slipping and sliding.

Sheri Van Oosten
Omaha, Nebraska

BUBBLE BATH

Ivory Liquid is the cheapest bubble bath and probably one of the gentlest!

Nancy Oberst
Omaha, Nebraska

BABY OIL

I put baby oil in my children's bath water to prevent dry skin.

Sally Lewis
Albuquerque, New Mexico

NO BABY SOAP

I found that baby soap dried my baby's skin, so
I use Neutrogena, which seems to keep his skin
softer.

Ann Louise Wolf
Newton, Massachusetts

BABY LOTION

I put Mennen Baby Magic Lotion on my babies'
bodies after each daily bath and diaper change. It
keeps them free of rashes and dry skin. As a bonus,
they smell nice all of the time!

Lois L. Mahowald
Omaha, Nebraska

Bathing Hints:
One-To Four-Year-Olds

BATH PLAYTIME

I allow my children plenty of playtime during the bath. We do the actual soaping at the very end. Also, I have learned that if I let all of the water out of the tub and then rinse the shampoo from the hair, there is less of a fuss.

Mary Jane DiChiacchio
Lansdowne, Pennsylvania

I bathe my 1½ and 3-year-olds together with bubble bath and their plastic toys. I find the 5:00 to 6:00 P.M. hour to be the best time for bath time. That seems to be the most restless time of the day for kids. The bath relaxes them and gives them something to do before dinner. It's a good time, too, to get them into their pajamas while you still have some energy left!

Debbie Karplus
Champaign, Illinois

FUN WASHING HAIR
  When washing my toddler's hair, we play a game
by using lots of suds and shampooing in front of a
mirror. We shape different hair-dos with the suds.
It's fun for both of us. Be sure to use a shampoo that
won't sting the eyes!

Mitzi Worley
Omaha, Nebraska

DISLIKES SHAMPOO
  My son Ben hates shampoo time. I make it easier
on him by placing a dry folded washcloth on his
forehead. I then take a half gallon pitcher with warm
rinse water and pour toward his back from the front
using the cloth to block the water from his face. No
water or soap goes into his face this way. I also give
him a mirror to hold to watch himself.
  Shampooing is still not Ben's favorite activity, but
it certainly has become an easier time for Ben's mom!

Authors
Omaha, Nebraska

FEAR OF THE TUB
  My daughter Ginger, who is two, became so afraid
of taking a bath that she would actually scream
"help" and cling to me.
  I didn't know what to do at first, but I finally decided to get into the tub with her and sit her on my lap.
Before long, she was playing with a cup in the water
and kicking her feet!

Mrs, Virginia Fallon
Turnersville, New Jersey

  My 1½-year-old daughter suddenly developed a
fear of the bath water. I tried putting only a little
water in the tub at a time. Each successive time I'd
put more water in until she was no longer afraid to
get in.

Authors
Omaha, Nebraska

KITCHEN SINK

For a fussy 2-year-old who refuses to take a bath in the tub, try letting him bathe in the kitchen sink. There are more things for him to look at and it saves having a fight. However, make sure he doesn't turn on the hot water and scald himself!

> *Nancy Oberst*
> *Omaha, Nebraska*

HAIR CUT

The best time to trim my toddler's hair has always been during his bath. His hair is already clean and wet, so it is easy to cut. The hair clippings come off with a simple rinse. Best of all, the bath toys keep him busy and still so I have both my hands free to shape and style.

> *Marsha Becker Sandersen*
> *Yakima, Washington*

HELP FROM DAD

My husband, Greg, wanted me to share with you the great experiences he has with Brian, such as bathing and changing his diapers. So many men consider this "woman's work" and I think that is so sad. Greg feels that if the husband shares these and other experiences with the child, the child will develop an even deeper bond with his dad.

> *Jeannine Adams*
> *Atlanta, Georgia*

DIAPERS AND OTHER DAILY MUST-DOS

Daily care of young ones would not be complete without some mention of the ENDLESS stream of dirty diapers. It's the kind of conversation topic that might have made you gag before you had children. After children, you suddenly find yourself chattering endlessly about your baby's latest bowel movement (or lack thereof), as if everyone will think it is fascinating news. To you and the baby, it is!

Even a woman who once swore she'd never do toilets, now handles far worse with relative ease. Every mom must face the fact that "poo-poo" is a major part of her job. You're a professional mother, so you handle it, although it's hard to imagine any other executive getting similar duty. The chairman of GE probably has never been called from a high-level meeting to change a pair of smelly pants. For that matter, some husbands cannot be coaxed from even a television commercial to handle a diaper change.

Cheer up though, because along with the diapers come lots of benefits, like receiving your child's hug or listening as the first gurgle of laughter leaves Baby's throat. When you think of those tender moments the job doesn't seem so bad and these hints will make it a little easier.

Diapering Hints

CORNSTARCH
We fill an empty shaker with cornstarch to use instead of baby powder. We shake it on after every diaper change. It is cheap, easy to refill, and it soothes Baby's irritated skin!

Ann Marie Williams
Philadelphia, Pennsylvania

I like to use cornstarch on my baby to prevent diaper rash. I have two glass jars with easy-to-open tops on my changing table. In one is cornstarch, and in the other, cotton balls. I just dip one of the balls in the cornstarch and powder him. It's a very simple process, and this way my baby doesn't inhale any powdery fumes.

Lynda Halbridge
Riverside, California

USING TWO CLOTH DIAPERS
Using regular cloth diapers for a baby is a chore when the baby wets through the diaper during the night. Try using a second diaper, folding it into thirds and placing it in the center of the other diaper (or just use two together). This way you don't have quite the mess to clean up in the morning.

Linda Larson
Troy, New York

BOTH CLOTH AND DISPOSABLE
I use cloth diapers regularly, but when we go out we use disposables. I keep some masking tape on hand, just in case Baby is still dry and the original tape is no longer useful. It's a shame to waste the whole dry paper diaper when masking tape does the trick!

Mrs. Shimon Soferr
Swampscott, Massachusetts

DIAPERING NEEDS

In General:

Diaper ointment
Cornstarch, baby powder, or lotion
Pre-moistened towelettes or wet cotton balls

Using Disposable Diapers
*note - check the various kinds of disposables to see which you prefer for your baby.

Diaper pail and plastic liners
4 waterproof pants (if you like)
1 dozen cloth diapers

Using Diaper Service
*note - a newborn uses about 80-100 diapers per week

1 dozen extra cloth diapers to supplement the diaper service
4 waterproof pants
1 box disposables per month for travel (if you want)
8 diaper pins (double locking heads)
Diaper liners

Laundering At Home

48 cloth diapers - if they're washed every other day
Diaper pail and plastic liners
8 diaper pins (double locking heads)
4 waterproof pants
1 box of disposables per month for travel
Diaper liners

HOW SHOULD I DIAPER MY BABY?

	Advantages	Disadvantages
DISPOSABLE DIAPERS	* No washing or folding * Very convenient, especially for travel * No diaper pins to buy * No worry about sticking Baby with pins * May not need to buy waterproof pants * Can buy different sizes to fit different sized bottoms	* Most expensive * Possibly a greater chance of developing diaper rash. One reason for this may be that disposables need not be changed as often * Inconvenience of having to go to store every time supply gets low * Not as soft as cloth diapers * Unlike cloth diapers, they cannot be "recycled"
DIAPER SERVICE	* Cheaper than disposables * Deodorized diaper pail and plastic liners are provided * A baby magazine is included and training pants are available * Diapers are delivered to your door * Professionally laundered and sanitized	* May still have to buy some disposables for travel * Have to change cloth diapers more frequently than disposables
HOME LAUNDERING	* Cheapest of all alternatives	* A lot of your time and effort spent on washing and folding * If not washed properly, bacteria can build up with each consecutive washing

DRYING PLASTIC PANTS

To dry plastic pants and keep them in good condition, I put them in the dryer after the other clothes are finished. I then run the dryer on the air cycle for ten minutes.

Rhonda Blum
Meraux, Louisianna

OTHER USES

I use disposable diapers for many things other than what they are made for. I use them to lie Baby on when changing her if I'm not at home, and as a lap protector when someone is holding her. It also doubles as a bib if I forget one.

Authors
Omaha, Nebraska

DIAPER RASH

To help prevent diaper rash:

1. Whenever you notice Baby's diaper is wet, change it as soon as possible.

2. Give your baby some water daily, because this helps dilute his urine.

3. After Baby's bath, don't put his diaper on right away. This allows his bottom more exposure to the air.

4. Periodically leave his rubber pants off. They do not allow air in.

5. After each bowel movement, wash your baby's bottom.

When redness first occurs:

1. Try a diaper rash ointment.

2. Leave the waterproof pants off for a day or so.

3. Feed your baby less fruit.

4. Expose Baby's bottom to air for longer periods of time.

5. Change Baby's diapers more often.

6. If you wash your baby's diapers, try a different detergent.

Call your doctor if none of these suggestions have worked after two days or so.

PAPER DIAPERS

For heavy wetters, use two paper diapers over each other at night. Put the first one on and put a large hole in the front, lower section. Then put the other diaper over that one. This allows the urine to pass into the next diaper without being stopped by the plastic.

Gail Zweigel
Atlanta, Georgia

If you're using paper diapers when baby's legs are so thin, (from birth to 3 months old), a Kotex placed in the diaper helps take up room and absorbs lots of liquid.

Beth Krewedl
Albuquerque, New Mexico

HOW TO WASH YOUR OWN DIAPERS

1. As soon as you change your baby's diaper, put it into a plastic pail filled with some water and 2 tbspn. of borax, and some well-disolved soap or detergent.

2. Stools must be dumped into the toilet. Rinse diaper while you flush the toilet.

3. Drain remaining water from the diaper pail.

4. Put diapers in Pre-soak cycle.

5. Wash in hot water with a mild detergent. Avoid fabric softeners and bleach because of potential for rash.

6. Rinse two or more times.

7. If you want to whiten the diapers, hang them on a line outside in the sun. However, automatic dryers are nice because they will soften diapers.

8. If you notice that your baby's diaper smells of amonia, you should take this extra step since amonia may cause diaper rash. Boil the diapers for 10-15 minutes before washing. Or use a diaper antiseptic in the last rinse. (Ask your doctor which one.) Vinegar may work.

CREATIVE DIAPER PAIL

Instead of using the standard diaper pail with the lid which you must pull off with your hand, get a plastic foot pedal garbage pail and put a stick-up deodorizer in it.

Gail Zweigel
Atlanta, Georgia

DIAPER PINS

I always put in diaper pins facing the baby's back. In case one should pop open, it won't stick your baby in a vital area.

Linda Vogel
Omaha, Nebraska

This idea was a lifesaver for me. I keep a large cake of Ivory soap (still in the wrapper) on my changing table to stick diaper pins in. It keeps the pins handy and they are much easier to pin through thick diapers.

Donna Hatfield
Monrovia, California

MOBILE OVER CHANGING TABLE

To corral an active squirming 8-month-old at diaper changing time, I hung a metallic fish mobile over the changing table, just out of his reach. The motion of his reaching arm would cause the mobile to move and he would stop wiggling long enough for me to pin on a diaper. By the way, his first word was "fish"!

Authors
Omaha, Nebraska

WINDOW VIEW

Our changing table is in front of a window. Ben loves to look out at the view while I change his diaper.

Donna Hatfield
Monrovia, California

CARD TABLE

I converted a card table into an excellent changing table. The table top is large enough to hold some diapers as well as the baby. This does require keeping your hand firmly on the baby at all times, as the table is light.

Alice Smith
Chicago, Illinois

IRONING BOARD

My husband and I couldn't afford new things for our baby, so instead of buying an expensive dressing table, I used my ironing board. The height is adjustable, it's wide enough for the baby, and it's already cushioned. Just don't let go of the baby the entire time she is on the ironing board.

Janet M. Parent
East Hartford, Connecticut

WET BAR

Our mobile home has a wet bar and we use it for our babies' changing table. We purchased a piece of foam rubber one inch thick to fit the countertop. Then we put on top a rubberized crib pad which had been cut to fit. We lay a towel over that because a towel can be changed easily and cleaned. The wet bar is backed by a mirror which keeps the boys amused during the diaper changes. All of their clothes and diaper supplies are stored in drawers and cabinets underneath, within easy reach. I keep fresh diapers on the shelves above.

Karen Leonard
Omaha, Nebraska

VANITY TOP

Use a vanity top as a changing table. Buy a table pad for the top. The mirror above the vanity will keep your baby entertained so it will be easy for you to change and dress him. My baby is 1 year old and still uses this table. We saved money by not buying a changing table, which babies quickly outgrow.

Keren Garcia
Monrovia, California

Feeding Time

Nothing erodes a mother's patience faster than feeding time. An infant who usually gulps down the formula in record speed suddenly becomes intent on sipping and savoring an ounce at a time. A toddler goes on a hunger strike. A nutrition-conscious mom rids her shelves of any product containing sugar, only to find that a kindly but misguided neighbor has turned the kids into lollipop junkies. Then there is the freshly washed baby who unloads mashed stew on her head. Have you ever tried to dig peas out of a young one's ears? All of these situations fall within the realm of an average day on the job of motherhood. Restoring the calm and friendly atmosphere the meal hour possessed before you had children may take some time. However, these hints just might help make it possible!

Nursing: Philosophies..................36

Nursing: How to Do it..................38

Bottle-feeding.........................42

Feeding Toddlers.......................43

Self-feeding...........................48

Clean-up...............................50

Nourishing Diet........................52

Fussy Eaters...........................55

Nursing: Philosophies

NURSING IS BEST

I had so much more confidence in my nursing the second time around. I nursed at every feeding. There is no need for sterilization, measuring, buying formula, and preparing it when you nurse. Occasionally I expressed my milk if I wasn't going to be home. I think nursing your baby is one of the best things you can do.

Authors
Omaha, Nebraska

DON'T LISTEN TO NEGATIVE COMMENTS

My best advice to a new nursing mom is don't listen to anyone who tells you that you won't be able to nurse your baby. Shut your ears when you hear: "The baby is crying because you don't have enough milk." I made the mistake of listening to others — mostly those who had never nursed — with my first baby and she weaned herself early because I supplemented with formula. Now, with my second child, I am still nursing and she is 10 months-old.

Authors
Omaha, Nebraska

NO TO NURSING

Breast-feeding was not for me. I felt I could be just as close to my baby by bottle-feeding him. Also, my husband could get up for the late night feedings to give me a break. One trick I learned was to switch arms when I fed the baby. I was told this helps with a baby's eye coordination.

Authors
Omaha, Nebraska

BOOKS ON BREASTFEEDING

THE WOMANLY ART OF BREASTFEEDING by the La Leche League International

NURSING YOUR BABY by Karen Pryor (Harper & Row)

BREASTFEEDING & NATURAL CHILD SPACING by Sheila Kippley (Harper & Row)

FEEDING NECESSITIES

If breast-feeding

Nursing bras
Nursing pads
Commercial breast cream or lanolin for sore nipples
*Breast pump (although expressing milk by hand works well)
8-ounce bottles (2 or more for juice and water)
4-ounce bottle (1)

If bottle-feeding

8-ounce bottles (8)
4-ounce bottles (4)
8 nipples and caps
Bottle and nipple brushes; or pre-sterilized disposable nurser kits
*Electric bottle warmer
To prepare formula at home: measuring cups and spoons, graduate
to mix formula, sterilizer and utensils.

When food is introduced

Baby dishes and utensils
*Feeder for strained foods
4 or more bibs
High chair or feeding table
*Food grinder
*Blender to make baby food

*May be nice to have but not necessary

Nursing: How To Do It

LA LECHE

When I was first nursing my son, I didn't know how to hand-express my milk into a bottle, so I called our local La Leche group. The number was in the phone book. The woman who answered was very helpful. I would not hesitate to call again.

Authors
Omaha, Nebraska

La Leche League•9616 Minneapolis Avenue•Franklin Park, Illinois 60131

DRINK, DRINK, DRINK

During my six months of nursing, I drank water or juice constantly to keep up my milk supply. Every time I thought of it, I'd drink a glass of water. I've read that it's also good to have liquid 10 to 15 minutes before nursing your baby.

Ann Louise Wolf
Newton, Massachusetts

CHANGE BREASTS

It's important to remember to switch the breast you start with when you nurse. I devised my own method of remembering by switching my wedding ring to my right or left hand, depending on which breast my son was to nurse on at his next feeding.

Authors
Omaha, Nebraska

HOW LONG ON EACH SIDE

When I nursed my baby his for first six months, I'd start on one side for about ten minutes, then let him nurse however long he wanted on the second side. At his next feeding, I'd start with the other breast (the one I had ended with). When Mark started solids at about six months of age, his nursing time decreased to about five minutes each side.

Authors
Omaha, Nebraska

WHEN TO NURSE

My son, David, would always fall asleep after being nursed. Therefore, I always nursed him before his nap-times. It made such a peaceful transition for him. After nursing, I would just lay him quietly in his crib.

Lynda Halbridge
Riverside, California

HAIR WASH WHILE NURSING

Newborns don't need a *full* bath very often, but you can keep them feeling a little fresher by using a warm washcloth to massage their heads while they are nursing. You will have a calm baby who won't squirm during the wash.

Donna Hatfield
Monrovia, California

INCLUDING AN OLDER CHILD

What do you do with your boisterous 3-year-old when you're breast-feeding your baby? My 3-year-old and I decided that this would be a special time for us, also. I would nurse the baby and read a story to my older child at the same time. That is one advantage of breast-feeding. You have a free hand for a hug, wipe of a child's nose, or whatever you want to do!

Authors
Omaha, Nebraska

When you have a toddler at home and a new baby, feeding time becomes quite a challenge. I give the older child a drink or snack before I breast-feed the baby, so we will not be interrupted for twenty minutes or so.

Carolyn Lyman
Potomac, Maryland

PHONE OFF THE HOOK

Nursing my son has a very relaxing and calming effect on me. To add to my tranquility, I take the phone off the hook. There is nothing worse for Mom and Baby than to be quietly nursing when the phone rings.

Authors
Omaha, Nebraska

BRA PADS

As a third-time breast-feeding mother, I have found that my husband's cotton handkerchiefs make very good bra pads. They don't cost anything extra, are reusable, and can be folded into a variety of thicknesses.

Jane Colmer
St. Joseph, Missouri

WHAT CLOTHES TO WEAR

Two-piece outfits, such as a blouse and pants, make the most convenient clothes for nursing. A layered outfit, like a jacket or vest also works well. I chose patterned fabrics because if my milk leaks, it doesn't show as much. Also, the pattern may hold some visual interest for my daughter as she nurses.

Authors
Omaha, Nebraska

NO MEDICATIONS

I avoided all medications while I was pregnant. It makes only common sense for me to do the same while I am nursing. I check with my doctor even before taking aspirin.

Lynda Halbridge
Riverside, California

DO NOT use nursing as a method of birth control.

NURSING IN PUBLIC

To solve the problem of exposure while nursing
in public, I loosely cover my shoulder and my baby
with a lightweight receiving blanket. No one can see
anything and I can even walk around holding my
baby while he is nursing.

Lynda Halbridge
Riverside, California

SORE NIPPLES

I had very sore nipples when I began to nurse. I
found that using a commercial breast cream helped.
I also avoided using soap on them. I aired the nipples after each feeding for ten minutes or so. Taking a hot shower and applying hot compresses helped
too. Eventually the soreness went away.

Authors
Omaha, Nebraska

NURSING SUBSTITUTE

My mother-in-law remembered this when she was
babysitting my inconsolable breast-fed baby. When
a nursing baby won't take a bottle from a sitter, try
a clean cloth napkin, dipped in sugar on the inside
and gathered up to form a corner. It's referred to
as a "sugar tit." Sometimes it will quiet the baby and
becomes a lifesaver for the sitter. Other times the
opinionated baby wants only the real thing, but it's
worth a try!

Kate Cavanaugh
Washington, D.C.

A BOTTLE SOMETIMES

I expressed my milk into a bottle for the occasional
times I went out. I think it was a good idea for Matthew to drink from a bottle once in awhile. Then if
there was an emergency and I couldn't be home, it
wouldn't be so traumatic for him.

Ann Louise Wolf
Newton, Massachusetts

Bottle-Feeding

READ LABELS

Be sure to read labels closely on formula cans. One time I was giving my baby the formula that should be diluted with water. I realized I had misread the label and had not added water. The can looked very similar to the ready-to-feed cans. Also check the expiration date.

Authors
Omaha, Nebraska

NYLON NET BAGS

The nylon net bags that wrap onions, potatoes, or other vegetables at the grocery store can be used as containers for washing nipples and bottle caps. You simply put the nipples, rings, and caps into the bag. Then throw the bag in the top of the dishwasher and wash away!

Sarah Gail Hytowitz
Norcross, Georgia

TWO BATCHES

To save some time, I make two batches of formula at one time. Pour one batch into bottles and keep one batch in a jar in the refrigerator.

Shirley Pitcher
Omaha, Nebraska

DID YOU KNOW that most formulas contain a combination of water, cow's milk and sugar?

MAKE IT EASIER

I lessen the hardship of those middle-of-the-night bottle feedings by keeping a ready-to-feed bottle at my bedside. All I have to do is twist off the lid, screw the nipple on, get my baby, and we're all set!

Authors
Omaha, Nebraska

BATTLE OF THE BOTTLE

I have heard again and again about the terrible trouble parents have when they try to wean their children from a bottle to cup. I avoided this problem by not allowing my children to use their bottles as a source of comfort or a plaything. I never gave the baby her bottle without holding her. This way she derived comfort and love from being held, rather than from the physical presence of her bottle. I believe mothers should take the time to hold their babies at feeding time, especially when they are infants. Do not hand the bottle to the baby or prop the bottle when the baby is tiny.

Barbara Arkin
Roselle, Illinois

Feeding Toddlers

FOOD IN A BOTTLE

At his evening feeding, my 3-month-old son ate cereal, but he needed more sucking. So I put his cereal in a 4-ounce bottle, and made the hole in the nipple a little bigger. Now he gets both the sucking and the cereal.

Janet M. Parent
East Hartford, Connecticut

MAKING MEALTIME PLEASANT

These feeding tips worked for me:

1) With a toddler, always keep her company while she eats, and use the time to talk. Encourage her to tell Daddy about her day.

2) With more than one child, don't compare.

3) Once in awhile, try eating in the dining room with candles and all. You'll be surprised at the improved table manners. We eat some dinner meals there with linen cloth and napkins. It's very pleasant.

Mary Jane DiChiacchio
Lansdowne, Pennsylvannia

REACT CALMLY

It's easy to get upset when babies cry, throw food, push over a vase, or just seem cranky for no reason. When you feel your temper rise, just keep telling yourself they are babies and don't know better. Don't get mad. Count slowly and then react calmly.

Mothers from New London
New London, New Hampshire

FOODS TO AVOID FOR CHILDREN UNDER 1½ YEARS

Difficult to Digest or May Cause Gagging

Raw Onion	Raw Carrot Sticks
Corn	Olives
Lettuce	Dried peas or Beans
Nuts	Popcorn
Raisins	Hard Candies

Not Nutritious

Any foods containing chocolate	Sugar-Coated Cereals
Cakes	Soft Drinks
Cookies	Kool Aid
Candies	Syrup
Pastries	Jelly

Other Foods to Avoid

Honey
Foods containing a lot of salt
Fatty foods
Artificial sweeteners
Coffee
Tea

A CHAIR WITH A VIEW

I feed my baby girl in her highchair, near my window overlooking the street. She loves seeing the cars, trucks, and buses go by.

Mrs. Shimon Soferr
Swampscott, Massachusetts

TEETHING

A frozen raw carrot was soothing on my baby's sore gums and easy to hold. When thawed, I refroze it and gave a new one to my baby. I kept a baggie with about six small pieces in my freezer.

Inez Davis
Kansas City, Missouri

I found that teething biscuits made a horrendous mess. So I use frozen bagels instead, which serve the same purpose with less clean-up.

Eileen Baron
Simsbury, Connecticut

POPSICLES

I make popsicles for my baby by pouring apple juice into an ice cube tray and freezing it. This serves a dual purpose. It feels good on his gums because he is teething and it makes a tasty treat without sugar!

Beth Ginsburg
Omaha, Nebraska

PREVENTING TOOTH DECAY

* Don't give your baby a pacifier that has been dipped in honey or sugar.
* Don't allow your child to go to sleep with a bottle.
* Limit your child's walking around with a bottle containing juice or milk.
* Clean teeth when they first come through. Consult your dentist or pediatrician for further information.

DOUBLE YOUR RECIPES

Whenever possible, make double quantities of food and freeze one. Then on one of those days when baby is sick or irritable and needs your special attention, you can just thaw a meal and warm it up!

Inez Davis
Kansas City, Missouri

EGG POACHER

An egg poacher is ideal for heating small portions of baby food without scorching or sticking. You can also lift out the top and use it as a plate to feed baby.

Connie Joanedis
Media, Pennsylvania

EASY BABY FOOD

The best way to feed a toddler is to grind up whatever food you had for your main meal and freeze it in the sections of an ice cube tray. Each section is enough for a meal. Just heat it up!

Linda Larson
Troy, New York

BABY FOOD FROM SCRATCH

I prefer to make my own baby food. One afternoon every two weeks or so, I cook vegetables, meat, etc. in quantity, and puree them in a blender separately. I add liquid or vegetable juice to each batch. Then I pour the mixture into an ice cube tray, thus making sixteen portions of adequate size for a new eater.

June Glazer
Ft. Worth, Texas

LEFTOVER BABY FOOD

I found a great use for baby food that is unopened. I bake with it. Carrot baby food is great in carrot cake and much easier to use because you don't have to shred the carrots. I'll continue to use it after my baby stops eating it. The banana baby food is also good in banana bread. Try anything!

Ann Louise Wolf
Newton, Massachusetts

AVERAGE BABY'S WEIGHT GAIN

1-3 months of age — about 2 pounds a month

6 months old   — about 1 pound a month

9-12 months   — about ⅔ pound a month

12-24 months   — about ½ pound a month

Average Baby's birthweight is double at around 5 months of age.

CHUNKY SOUP

If your baby is just beginning to eat table foods, an undiluted can of "Chunky" beef vegetable soup makes an easy and balanced meal.

Debby Shepherd
Birmingham, Alabama

HOT DOGS AND BISCUITS

For 2-year-olds and up, try this fun to eat meal. Cut hot dogs in half and roll each in a Pepperidge Farm biscuit. Bake them about fifteen minutes or until the biscuits are golden brown.

Another fun food for kids is pancakes made about the size of a quarter. Cookies can also be made that small for easy holding and eating.

Mothers from New London
New London, New Hampshire

APPLIANCES

I have found that a blender, pressure cooker, and a juicer are very useful appliances for preparing food for a toddler. I buy whole cases of fruit in season, especially apples, and make fresh juices.

Debbie Karplus
Champaign, Illinois

GIVE THEM A CHOICE

As soon as my oldest child was 1½, I let him tell me what he wanted to eat. I'd also ask, "Do you want a lot or a little?" and he would tell me. He would always clean his plate because he was served exactly what he wanted. Too permissive? I don't think so. I only gave him quality foods to choose from, no candy or desserts. Over a three day period, he would choose a totally balanced diet. For example, one day all of his choices would be high protein type foods like yogurt, cheese, peanut butter, soy bean curd, and so on. The next day he would pick lots of fruits and vegetables. Kids need to be given as much responsibility as they can handle in a controlled, structured setting. I think that's the trick!

Debbie Karplus
Champaign, Illinois

DRY MILK

Keep a box of instant non-fat dry milk around the house for emergencies or travel.

Gail Zweigel
Atlanta, Georgia

Self-Feeding

SHOT GLASS

When my children began drinking from a cup, I gave them a shot glass. It's just the right size for small hands to hold.

Linda Reickert
Castleton, New York

FRUIT COCKTAIL

If your new table food eater wants to feed herself, try chunky fruit cocktail. This works very well for a beginner.

Debby Shepherd
Birmingham, Alabama

MASHED POTATOES

When your child is ready to feed himself with a
spoon, start with mashed potatoes. They won't slip
off the spoon as most other foods do.

Authors
Omaha, Nebraska

FINGER FOODS

When my 8-month-old doesn't want to eat his
strained food, I've found giving him some sort of
finger food works well. A small piece of bread or a
cracker seems to work the best. Occasionally, he enjoys a hot dog or a meat stick when that is what his
older sister is having.

I also try to make his meal as close to what his
sister is having, such as giving him a little mashed
potato, cut up carrots or any other soft-cooked
vegetables. Be sure to omit salt and use very little
butter.

Mrs. Wm. D. Pearson
Rockford, Illinois

DISH WITH A PEDESTAL

When a child is first learning to feed himself, give
him a dish on a pedestal. It brings the food closer
to him and he will be able to hold onto the dish
better.

Dorothy Mohl
Troy, New York

TWO SPOONS

For a toddler, learning to use a spoon for self-
feeding can be made easier through this method: I
call it the Two-Spoon approach. I use one spoon for
her to handle, then I fill the second spoon with food.
Finally I take the empty spoon in exchange for the
full one. This way she has to put a full spoon into
her mouth, but she doesn't have to load it.

Ann Marie Williams
Philadelphia, Pennsylvania

SOME FINGER FOODS FOR CHILDREN 9 MONTHS AND OLDER

Fresh Vegetables: cooked and cut up: broccoli, cauli-
                          flower, potatoes, carrots

Fresh Fruit: peel and cut up into small pieces:
                          bananas, apples, nectarines, pears,
                          peaches, plums, canteloupe, seeded
                          watermelon, orange and grapefruit
                          sections, avocado

Meats: cut into small pieces: hamburger,
                          lamb chops, tuna fish, turkey, liver,
                          roast, meatballs

Breads: Whole wheat bread and toast, cook-
                          ed macaroni, cheerios, muffins

Dairy: Cottage cheese, hard boiled and
                          scrambled eggs (start with the yolk),
                          deviled eggs, and mild natural cheese
                          (cut up)

Clean-Up

BEACH TOWEL

When your child is learning to feed himself, place
a large beach towel under the highchair. This will
expedite clean-up of the floor. All you have to do is
shake it out. Then at the end of the day when your
child goes to sleep, throw the towel into the wash.

Stefani Roth
Houston, Texas

SHOWER CURTAIN LINER

We bought a shower curtain liner for $4.50 to put
under our toddler's feeding chair. The liner catches
the food and the liquid from her cup and it sure saves
on carpet cleaning!

Ann Marie Williams
Philadelphia, Pennsylvania

USE NEWSPAPER

Spread newspaper under highchairs for easy clean-up after the meal.

Deborah Gans
Goleta, California

BOWL OF WATER

Most babies don't like to have their faces and hands washed after meals. I have solved the problem with my son. Since he was 5 months old, I have brought a finger bowl filled with warm water to his highchair after he eats. He loves to dip his hands into it. This method gets his hands much cleaner than just wiping with a wash cloth. My son is now three and to this day he doesn't mind getting his hands cleaned in this manner.

Barb Wadleigh
Madison, Wisconsin

PLACE MAT

The highchair tray is a mess to clean after your toddler mashes all of the food around. Here is an easy way to keep an old or new highchair tray cleaner. Take a plastic place mat (about 50¢) and cut it to the shape of the tray. Be sure to cut the place mat a bit smaller than the tray so it fits in easily, but not so loose that it slides around. Sometimes it helps to trace a pattern out of an old grocery sack and then cut the place mat.

Then when your baby makes a mess, simply take off the mat and give it a good washing in the sink. Food comes right off! This trick makes old highchairs usable again because you have a nice clean tray surface that is washable.

Ellyn Gunness
Needham, Massachusetts

PLASTIC

Put a piece of plastic under the highchair so that when food is spilled, all you have to do is pick up the plastic and throw the food into the trash.

Mothers from New London
New London, New Hampshire

PLASTIC BIBS
When our son turned a year old, I decided I was through washing ten bibs every other day. So I discovered the molded plastic bibs. They're great! All of the food is caught in the bib, and you just rinse it off in the sink!

Authors
Omaha, Nebraska

MOM'S BIB
I get so messy while feeding my baby his food, that I now wrap a lightweight towel around my neck and use it as my own bib.

Authors
Omaha, Nebraska

Happy Birthday 1-Year-Old!

Baby probably has:
* tripled his birth weight

* grown one-third of his birth length

* 6 to 8 teeth

Nourishing Diet

AVOIDING SWEETS
If you don't want your child to be a sweet freak, do the obvious. Don't keep sweets around the house! A youngster will probably look forward to eating ice cream and cake at birthday parties, but if there is none of it at home, he can't eat it, so he won't be tempted.

If you find *you* have to eat sweets, why not do it while your child is sleeping? You can control yourself until his nap or until he goes to sleep for the night. After all, you are forming life-long habits in your child's diet.

Authors
Omaha, Nebraska

VEGETARIAN DIET

Whatever Mom and Dad are eating, kids can eat too! We are long-time vegetarians on a no sugar, no additives, natural foods diet and it suits the kids well. Meals are easy. Apple slices covered with peanut butter and a glass of milk make a simple yet nutritious lunch. Dinner might be a larger meal, perhaps salad, cooked veggies, and a cheese or nut casserole for protein.

Debbie Karplus
Champaign, Illinois

JUICE

When I run out of milk or when my children are on a milk-restricted diet, I pour fruit juice over their cereal. Wesley is three and loves juice (without added sugar) on Wheaties.

Sally Lewis
Albuquerque, New Mexico

CEREAL

At age 2, Jen still eats the baby iron-fortified cereal. I see no reason to take her off it. She still likes the taste and there is no salt or sugar added to it, so it's very good for her. Now that Jen is older, she adds a few Cheerios to her cereal.

Authors
Omaha, Nebraska

RICE PUFFS

For a snack, I feed my 9-month-old rice puffs from the health food store. This snack is much more nutritious than processed cereals which are full of preservatives and sugar.

Mrs. Richard A. Johnson
Goleta, California

Don't overfeed your Baby. There is evidence to support the theory that fat babies become fat children who in turn become fat adults.

CINNAMON FOR FLAVOR

My daughter will eat almost anything if I add a little spice to it. She wouldn't touch cottage cheese and toast until I added a little cinnamon on top of the sandwich. Now, it is one of her favorite luncheon treats. This way I avoid using sugar in her diet, but the food is far from bland.

Deborah Levin-Brown
Miami Beach, Florida

ADD WHEAT GERM

To add fiber to my little one's diet, I add a little wheat germ to his baby cereal. Wheat germ can also be thrown into a toddler's meal for added nutrition.

Lynda Halbridge
Riverside, California

WEIGHT WATCHING

I do the following things to curtail my child's weight gain: 1) I cut down on his desserts and snacks. I give him a piece of fruit (without added sugar) instead of cakes or cookies. Grapefruit or strawberries are delicious, nonfattening desserts and snacks. 2) When we go out to dinner with our son, I bring along a non-fattening cracker, such as London Melba Toast for him to munch on. 3) We also avoid the sugar-frosted or honey-coated types of cereals.

Authors
Omaha, Nebraska

ADDED NUTRITION

Meatloaf is a great dish in which to hide healthy food. Just follow your regular recipe but add anything your child does not like or is not getting enough of. I throw in apple sauce, an egg, mashed vegetables, wheat germ. almost anything! My daughter gobbles it up!

If you use a grinder or a food processor to blend the ingredients, the loaf will be easier for a little one to eat.

Authors
Omaha, Nebraska

YOGURT TREAT
    I don't buy the yogurt with fruit because it contains sugar. Instead, I buy plain yogurt and baby food fruit (without added sugar). I mix the two together. My son and I both love it.
Lynda Halbridge
Riverside, California

CHOLESTEROL
    If you are watching your child's cholesterol intake and you still want to serve eggs, you can try "white scrambled eggs." You make scrambled eggs but eliminate one or two of the yokes.
Authors
Omaha, Nebraska

CHOKING PREVENTION
* Don't let your child walk or run if he's eating.

* Calm him down when he gets playful and excited during mealtime.

* Be sure and cut all food into very small pieces.

* Instruct your child to chew slowly and carefully.

Fussy Eaters

MALTS
    For babies who are picky eaters, prepare malteds with an egg, yogurt, fruit and milk. They'll love it!
Gail Zweigel
Atlanta, Georgia

    Our children, ages 20 months and 3½ years have had times when they didn't seem to eat enough to keep a bird alive. When that happens, we try to start their day right with a "Morning Malt": one cup of milk, one egg, three tablespoons of malt and a flavoring.
Diana Hill
Azusa, California

FRUIT IN CEREAL
When the time comes when your infant likes fruit
better than cereal, try mixing the two together. It
is more filling and nourishing.

Linda Larson
Troy, New York

DID YOU KNOW eating spoonfuls of peanut butter straight from the jar is
dangerous? Dr. Henry Heimlich knows of two cases in which people have
choked to death from doing this.

SUBSTITUTING MEAT
To provide extra protein for a baby (6-12 months
old) who doesn't like meat, I melt about one table-
spoon of peanut butter in warm milk and mix it with
baby cereal. My baby loves it.

Connie Joanedis
Media, Pennsylvania

MIXING FOOD
When Jen was about 14 months old and didn't like
what we were eating, I would try mixing some food
that she did like with the food that she didn't like.
For example, I'd try a small portion of ground beef
mixed with applesauce (no sugar added) or tuna fish
mixed with sour cream.

Authors
Omaha, Nebraska

CHOICES
Cut up the favorite and not so favorite foods into
bite-sized snacks for lunch and let the toddler choose
which ones to eat. He usually ends up trying
everything.

Donna K. Short
Omaha, Nebraska

CLOWN FACES

Make happy clown or sad clown faces on food for your fussy child at mealtime. Use raisins or grapes for eyes and noses. A canned cheese spread can help create interesting faces on sandwiches or soups. I even use ketchup to make a face on hamburgers.

I also write our son's name on food or make other simple shapes as the food permits, such as making jack-o-lantern faces in peaches or apples.

Authors
Omaha, Nebraska

EGG CARTON LUNCH

Lunch is a difficult meal for me to fix because I seem to make the same things over and over. So I thought of an "egg carton" lunch. I save empty egg cartons and I put a different finger food in each hole: carrot pieces, cheese slices, crackers, bread, fresh vegetables, chicken pieces and so on. My son always has a lot of fun with this lunch and he seems to eat things he normally would not try.

Authors
Omaha, Nebraska

LUNCH BOX

For a fun eating experience at home, pack your toddler's lunch in a bag or a lunch box. My toddler loves to eat this way and it is very convenient for me because I then have time to sit and feeds the baby without jumping up every few minutes to get something to amuse the toddler.

Margie Gutnik
St. Louis, Missouri

CREATIVE COOKERY

When I make pancakes for children older than two, I pour the batter on the skillet and make different shapes such as dogs, snakes, bunny heads, triangles, and footballs. It's not hard to do without cutters. Also, I cut sandwich bread into different shapes, although I use cutters for this. Kids think it is more fun to eat this way!

Mitzi Worley
Omaha, Nebraska

ADD SAUCE

Have you ever tried fish sticks for finger food? We also found that a little catsup or barbeque sauce on chicken, turkey, fish, etc. like Mommy and Daddy use, made a non-eater's meal acceptable!

Lisa Ginsburgh
Schaumburg, Illinois

OMELET

For a fussy eater, try this tiny-tot omelet. Beat one egg. Add 3-5 teaspoons milk. Cook in a small frying pan. When the omelet begins to set, add tiny cooked potato cubes, finely diced tomato bits, and a few alfalfa sprouts. Remember, *no* salt! For a variation try tiny cheese cubes instead of potato.

Jane Price
Vancouver, Washington

LET JUNIOR FIX IT

I find that my 4-year-old, who's a finicky eater, will eat almost anything if I let him make it. I just close my eyes to the mess and clean it up later. His favorite foods to make are tuna salad, egg salad, bologna sandwiches, meat loaf, and tossed salad.

Margie Gutnik
St. Louis, Missouri

LUNCHTIME EXCITEMENT

To make an exciting lunch for a fussy eater:

1) Make a small nest with grated carrots and fill the nest with raisins or peanuts.

2) Slice thin apple slices to dip into a small paper cup of yogurt sprinkled with cinnamon.

3) Cut bread with animal cookie cutters and spread with a mixture of mashed banana and peanut butter.

4) Add a teaspoon or two of molasses to a cup of milk and serve it in a small root beer mug.

Jane Price
Vancouver, Washington

Household Organization???

Babies and toddlers are natural "messers." Their curiosity turns your entire home into a playpen. Blocks find their way into every room. Stuffed animals peek out of every corner. If you're brave enough to leave knick-knacks on the coffee table, don't be surprised to find them later, floating in the toilet. Your toddler was simply launching an imaginary fleet!

Discouraging? Absolutely. You could just resign yourself to the idea that a neat house is boring to a little one and that chaos is creative. If you and your husband can accept that, you can skip this chapter. Just draw your curtains and lock the door when a finicky relative comes to call. However, if you still like to leaf through *House Beautiful* and dream of rooms free of clutter, then follow these hints faithfully. We can't bring miracles, but if you've got an active and curious toddler, you'll probably be grateful for any improvement!

Organizing............................61

Making Dinner........................66

Organizing Clothes....................68

Decorating Baby's Room...............69

Organizing

GARBAGE PAILS

I've found that plastic garbage pails in different colors can be used to keep toys from getting under foot. In one pail I throw all the cars, in another pail I put small toys, and in a third go all the dolls. Pick-up goes quickly and it's easy to find any certain toy. The pails make a darling and inexpensive set of toy boxes.

Deborah Sawyer
Dracut, Massachusetts

STORAGE BINS

The solid, plastic, stacking, vegetable storage bins make dandy storage for small toys. We use them in our Headstart classroom for small cars, trucks, doll house furniture, and small blocks. Children enjoy putting the toys in their places.

Diana Hill
Azusa, California

LAUNDRY BASKET

For an inexpensive toy box, turn an old laundry basket into a keeper of your child's toys.

Suzanne Luter
Omaha, Nebraska

DIAPER BOXES

As your child's toys multiply, sort out the old ones they have outgrown every few months and store them in large cardboard diaper boxes for your next child.

Gail Zweigel
Atlanta, Georgia

WICKER BASKETS

Organizing all of my 8-month-old's little things has become an absolute necessity and a real challenge! I've taken advantage of the decorative and useful wicker baskets which come in a variety of sizes and shapes. I use a small wicker basket for storing and transporting soap and other bath articles to and from the nursery and bath. I use a large laundry basket for collecting and transporting things up and down the stairs.

Denise Clapman
Eagle Mills, New York

STORING PUZZLES

Toys with many pieces always pose a problem and puzzles are probably the worst! Color-code each puzzle and include the number of pieces each contains. Frameless cardboard puzzle pieces can be easily stored in plastic margarine tubs.

Marsha Becker Sandersen
Yakima, Washington

SORTING TOYS IN THE MORNING

To help keep my girls' bedroom neat, along with instilling good habits in them, I put a medium-sized cardboard box under one bed. Every evening right before bedtime any toys, books, cards, or other items lying on the floor are put in the box by the girls. Then in the morning, we go through the box and sort the toys into their proper places, This has eliminated a lot of tired whining at night when the girls don't feel like doing the extra work.

Jane Colmer
St. Joseph, Missouri

USE DRAWERS IN EACH ROOM

If every room of your home is littered with toys by the end of the day, empty a drawer in each room and store toys in them. This saves time because you won't have to haul toys back to one area.

Authors
Omaha, Nebraska

TOO MANY PIECES

Many toys with multiple parts, such as a set of blocks come in boxes that can't be closed once they are opened. My children have so many toys with parts that when they are thrown into the toy box, they hardly get used at all. I solved the problem by taking scraps of leftover fabric, lace, and ribbon and making drawstring bags with monogrammed pictures of the toys on them.

All the bags are hung neatly on pegs on the wall and my daughter Stacie can see the pictures and is learning what toys go where. The bags are easy for even 2-year-olds to carry and toy parts aren't scattered all over.

Cindi Schaub
Azusa, California

BATH TOYS

Store bath toys in a wire vegetable basket. It can be hung from the shower head so the toys can airdry and not mildew. The basket can also be easily removed to hang on a towel rod while adults use the shower. A fish net sack will serve the same purpose.

Diana Hill
Azusa, California

I bought a plastic bicycle basket to keep my children's bath toys in. It attaches over our towel rack.

Patty Sherman
Omaha, Nebraska

SPECIAL PLACES FOR BOOKS

We have certain spots for Jennifer's books, different from where her toys are. In our family room, she has one portable book shelf which lies on the floor. In her bedroom, she has a book rack on her dresser. We try to teach her that books are very special and should be put back where they belong after we're done reading them.

Authors
Omaha, Nebraska

DOING A LITTLE SAVES A LOT

I learned to do little things all of the time to avoid a pile-up of chores. For example, I pick up the bathroom while my baby sits in her infant seat on the floor. She loves to watch me.

In general, I have to give up having a meticulously clean house so I can just take time to enjoy my baby. I simply ignore the unnecessary feelings of guilt over a living room that hasn't been vacuumed today.

Inez Davis
Kansas City, Missouri

As a mother of 7-month-old twins, I have found this time-saver. Don't try to clean the whole house in one day. Instead clean one room each day. Monday, do the living room. Tuesday, the dining room. Wednesday, the laundry room. This method really helps and you don't drag yourself to bed at night.

Pam Luiten
Duarte, California

HELPFUL HANDS

The older children think housework is a game, so I save chores for when they are up and need something to do.

Jane Colmer
St. Joesph, Missouri

MAKING A LIST

On Sunday night, I compile a list of everything I foresee being done in the coming week. I then break up the chores by day according to importance so I know just what I should get accomplished each day. Then my weekends are pretty much free.

Lois L. Mahowald
Omaha, Nebraska

KEEP A RELAXED SCHEDULE

Moms should plan no more than one major activity for the day to avoid becoming rushed. For example, if you are preparing a week's worth of casseroles for the freezer that day, then don't plan a shopping trip, house cleaning, or visitors. If you happen to have time left over, then do the extras. By not scheduling yourself too tightly, the atmosphere of your home will stay relaxed and friendly.

Debbie Karplus
Champaign, California

DON'T PULL YOUR HAIR OUT WHEN "JUNIOR" OR "MISSY":

* decides to mash *GUM* into overalls instead of chewing it.
ANTIDOTE - Use ice to harden gum, scrape off as much as possible, add stain remover, then wash.

* draws a picture with *CRAYON* on a new outfit.
ANTIDOTE - Use soap and water on stain then wash in hottest water fabric can take.

* leaves more green on the seat of his or her pants than is left in the *GRASS.*
ANTIDOTE - Scrub stain with detergent and water then wash in hottest water fabric can take. If the green still won't come out, gently rub with alcohol, rinse with water and wash again.

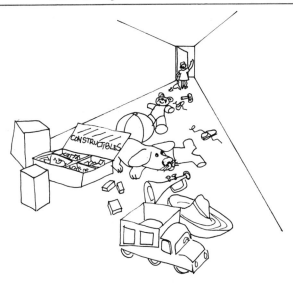

Making Dinner

INFANT SEAT

If you have an infant up to 3 months of age, and there is ample room with safety, put him in an infant seat and place the seat on the counter while you do dishes or cook. I found my baby would sleep if I turned on the kitchen exhaust fan while cooking or if I ran the dishwasher.

Alice Smith
Chicago, Illinois

I put Baby in his infant seat on the cupboard beside me. As I opened cans of chopped vegetables and other goodies, I would let him smell and have small tastes of certain appropriate foods. Not only did he enjoy watching and touching different things, but I enjoyed his responses, also!

Shauna Petersen
Kearns, Utah

When using an infant seat, be sure to tie the strap around your baby. You never know when your infant will make his first move and fall out of the seat.

KITCHEN CABINET

I gave my child her own cupboard in the kitchen to keep her busy while I prepare dinner. She can play in her Cubby anytime, as there are only pots, pans, and other non-breakables in it. She thinks she's helping with dinner by banging the pans. She really is!

Kathy Hungate
Goleta, California

PREPARING DINNER IN THE MORNING

I have found an easy way to fix dinner. After the baby's morning feeding, I prepare dinner for my husband and myself by using our crockpot. This gives me some extra time for other things.

Pam Luiten
Duarte, California

With 8 children, all under the age of 14, preparing the evening meal is a very hectic time for me! I try to get a head start by preparing as many dishes as I can in the morning before I clean up the breakfast dishes.

I make the jello or tossed salad, scrub and wrap the potatoes, clean and cut up vegetables, make the meatloaf, and refrigerate all of this until it is dinnertime. This saves me a lot of time and frustration.

Bonnie Campbell
Mesa, Arizona

MAKE DINNER AS THEY NAP

I often fix dinner when my children take their afternoon nap. Then I reheat it in the microwave oven before supper.

Rhonda Blum
Meraux, Louisianna

Organizing Clothes

DRESS UP

The night before a holiday or other occasion requiring special clothes, I put out all of the children's clothes in separate piles for each child. Each pile includes everything the child could possibly need, such as underwear, tights, shoes, hair ribbons, and hairbrushes. This simplifies things in the morning because there is no frantic last minute looking!

Kate Cavanaugh
Washington, D.C.

USING ALL SIZES

My daughter's clothing is put away in her dresser drawers according to size. Larger sizes are put on the bottom with the smaller ones on top. It's easy to misjudge the size of an outfit or even forget it completely, if it is tucked away in the back of a drawer. This way I know exactly where each outfit is and she gets good use out of all of them.

Jody Bomba
Monrovia, California

ORGANIZING DRAWERS

I put the clothes my baby wears every day in her top dresser drawer. Dressier clothes are in her second drawer. Outgrown items are at the bottom and when that drawer is too full I pack them up, label the box and put the box in her closet.

Authors
Omaha, Nebraska

OUTGROWN CLOTHES

I keep empty boxes in my baby's closet. When she grows out of her clothes, I put them in a box and seal it tight. On the outer side of the box, I make a list of what is inside such as pajamas, summer things, or shoes. I included the size of the clothes. When I have my second baby, I'll know exactly what is in the boxes and will have to unpack only what I need.

Charlene Baker
Thousand Oaks, California

Decorating Baby's Room

VISUAL STIMULI IMPORTANT
If you have a plain plastic crib bumper pad, use contact paper to create shapes to stick on the bumper pad. If you have a fabric bumper pad, use stitch-witchery fabric adhesive and iron on interesting calico shapes for visual interest.

Authors
Omaha, Nebraska

POSTERS
We were on a tight budget when it came to decorating the baby's room so we bought large posters of animals and tacked them on the wall. Ben is only a few weeks old but he loves to look at the colors. Contrasting colors like a dark panda bear against the white wall really fascinate him. Soon he'll be able to recognize the different animals. The animals will be appropriate for his room for years.

Donna Hatfield
Monrovia, California

NURSERY EQUIPMENT

Basic Items:
Crib
Mattress
Crib bumper pad
Bassinet
Chest of drawers
Dressing or changing table
Laundry hamper
Diaper pail

Decorative Items:

Nursery Lamp
Crib mobile
Growth chart
Wall pin-ups or pictures
Night Light
Unbreakable mirror

Later Additions

Table and Chair set
Toy Box
Foot Stool

WALLPAPER

I like bright, colorful wallpaper for a nursery, preferably wallpaper with animals and numbers on it. As I change my baby's diapers, I point out the name of each object on the paper. Changing diapers becomes a fun learning experience!

Jeannine Adams
Atlanta, Georgia

SIBLING ARTWORK

We wanted to include our older children in the decorating of our baby's room. They decided to draw some pictures for their new baby brother. We framed the pictures and hung them up on the wall above the crib. Our kids felt proud and the baby loved looking at them!

Authors
Omaha, Nebraska

MOBILES

I made a mobile out of pieces of felt and bright colored ribbons. I hung it from the dining room light within baby's reach. When we wanted a change, we moved the mobile into Baby's room for an added decoration.

Shirley Pitcher
Omaha, Nebraska

My husband and our 3-year-old daughter made a mobile of model planes for our baby. I hung the mobile over the changing table. This makes a great diversion during diaper changes. I feel it's far more useful there than over the crib.

Mrs. Shimon Soferr
Swampscott, Massachusetts

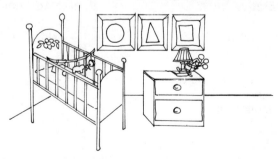

POM-POMS

Make bright-colored pom-poms out of four or five different colors of yarn. Three inches in diameter is a good size for the pom-poms. Use them for tossing games or hang them in mobile fashion. They are good for both visual and tactile stimulation. Just make sure the pom-poms are secure enough not to be pulled apart and eaten by your curious little one!

Authors
Omaha, Nebraska

PHOTOS

In my son's room I tacked pictures of his relatives on a bulletin board to help him remember them. Of course he loves to see himself in the pictures. It makes a colorful decoration and gives him the sense of belonging to a family.

Helen Cain
Omaha, Nebraska

When decorating my 2-year-old's room, I found that her favorite objects were pictures of herself. I made attractive frames by taking a piece of wood and sanding it smooth. I then cut out a picture of my child and put it on the wood. Over that I added three or four coats of decoupage glue. A nice finishing touch was achieved by cutting out her name from a pretty piece of wrapping paper and gluing it on. She just loves to see this on the wall!

Gayle Collins
Omaha, Nebraska

MACRAME

I made macrame animals and hung them on my baby's wall. They're cute, washable, and can be used over and over again.

Gail Furman
Springfield, Virginia

VELCRO TAPE

My first child got so many stuffed animals that we didn't know what to do with them. So I bought some Velcro tape and taped some strips onto one wall in his room, and stuck the animals onto the tape. It looks adorable, and he especially loves it now that he is older because he can easily play with them and put them back.

Authors
Omaha, Nebraska

SELECTING CARPET

When selecting carpet for a nursery, remember that a carpet with strands of mixed colors will be better for hiding stains than a monochromatic carpet.

Authors
Omaha, Nebraska

I would not recommend putting shag carpet in Baby's room. When we moved into our home, our little boy's room had shag carpet and all sorts of little objects became hidden in it. This was dangerous for our 7-month-old, as he would always find these objects and try to put them in his mouth.

Authors
Omaha, Nebraska

KITES

Bright cloth kites make beautiful room decorations! Later on they can be taken down and enjoyed by your child.

Sarah Gail Hytowitz
Norcross, Georgia

On The Move

Trip Preparation.......................74

Air Travel..........................76

Car Travel..........................77

Shopping............................85

Visiting In-Town.....................86

Dining Out..........................87

Trip Preparation

BAGGIES

Before going on a long trip, pack the clothes your child will be wearing in separate plastic bags for each day. For example, put in one bag a clean t-shirt, shorts, a top, a hat, and socks; all to be worn on Monday. The bags help you keep a neat suitcase and the clothes are easy to find. You don't have to dig through a suitcase to find a certain pair of socks anymore! As a bonus, the clothes will stay less wrinkled. The bags can also be used to store dirty clothes after each day's use, so there is less chance of clothes being accidentally discarded and left behind in hotel rooms. Another advantage is that when the child starts dressing himself, it is easier for him to find the clothes. This idea can be used as the children grow by just increasing the size of the plastic bags as the clothes get bigger.

Nancy String
Lakewood, Ohio

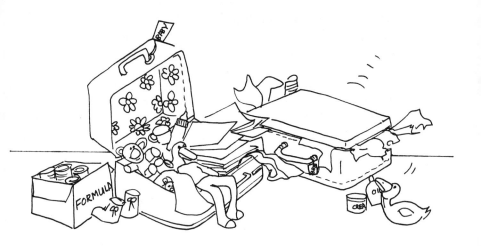

PLASTIC PRODUCE BAGS

Plastic produce bags from the supermarket provide excellent storage on trips and they're free. They come in handy for holding dirty diapers, leaky bottles, baby food jars, and wet clothing.

Janis Woodward
Monrovia, California

FAMILIAR ITEMS

When going on a trip with Baby, take along familiar blankets or toys for the crib, so the baby won't feel so strange in a different bed.

Sarah Gail Hytowitz
Norcross, Georgia

MEDICINES

Be sure to take a box full of medicines with you on your trip. You should include aspirin, cough syrup, a thermometer and band aids in this box. Besides being a great help in emergencies, this saves a trip to the pharmacy.

Mothers from New London
New London, New Hampshire

Air Travel

RESERVE BULKHEAD SEATING

On our airplane trip with my 11-month-old, I requested bulkhead seating, which is the first row after the first class partition. I didn't have to worry about the baby bothering anyone sitting in front of her. In flight she was able to sit on the floor with her favorite blanket and doll because this area has much more leg room than any other row.

Stefani Roth
Houston, Texas

If you travel with an infant and are lucky enough to receive bulkhead seating, be sure to ask for the bassinet which fits right into the wall. You must request this before you go on the plane, and remind the attendants again once you board. This way your infant will be able to sleep while you travel.

Aveva Shukert
Omaha, Nebraska

LABEL YOUR CHILD

When we travel by air, we always put a label on our toddler. We never expect to become separated, but we don't want to take that chance. We put her name, address, telephone number and flight number on the label.

Authors
Omaha, Nebraska

PLUGGED-UP EARS

Since little ears can get plugged-up when riding in an airplane, you should do any of the following to remedy the situation. You can nurse or bottle-feed your baby during the take-off and while descending. When the child gets older, you can give him something to eat during these times. Cheerios or apple slices do the trick. Give the child just enough food to make him swallow and his ears will unplug.

Lynda Halbridge
Riverside, California

TAKE A WALKER
   If you're taking a long trip and your baby is at the stage in which he needs a highchair, take the walker instead. It doubles nicely as a feeding chair if you brace the wheels with your feet. Best of all, it folds up very compactly and leaves you packing room for something else, like your *own* clothes! If the airline has a weight limit, this will help since a walker is much lighter than a highchair.

Authors
Omaha, Nebraska

Car Travel

NAP DURING TRIP
   Plan your driving time on a long trip to coincide with your children's nap schedule. Our daughters like the motion of the car to lull them to sleep. The nap makes their time spent cooped up in our car seem a little shorter.

Nancy Jacobson
Lincoln, Nebraska

TRAVEL AT NIGHT
   I recommend travelling at night with little ones. They'll probably sleep more, and you won't have to be changing diapers and entertaining them as much as during day travel. I also would suggest nursing on long trips, because you have warm milk on hand instantly.

Susan M. Sperry
Hunter, Utah

RAISE THE CAR SEAT
   Consider raising the car seat to its upright position when your infant is not supposed to nap. We realized that in its lowered position, all that Adam could see was the dashboard. Once he was higher and could see out the windows, he was much happier.

Lisa Ginsburgh
Schaumburg, Illinois

CAR SAFETY

Car accidents are the leading cause of death for children 1-4 years old. Unfortunately, most of these deaths could have been prevented. Most of the time, the youngster was not properly restrained in a safety device. Here are some preventive measures for your child.

SAFETY IN THE CAR

* Don't start the car unless everyone is buckled up, including Mom.
* When your car is moving, don't let your child stand on the seat or jump around.
* Always lock the car doors while in the car.
* Keep the window by your children closed.
* NEVER let your child play with the car controls.
* NEVER leave your children in the car by themselves.
* NEVER allow your child to ride in a car on an adult's lap.
* Car beds or bassinets do not protect your baby.
* When your child is riding with another person, instruct him to ask for protection in their car.

CAR RESTRAINTS

* Use a safety restraint *every time* your child is in the car. NO EXCEPTIONS. Start when your baby comes home from the hospital.
* Mom must use a seat belt too. Remember you're a role model for your child.
* Use the restraint in the back seat of the car. The *safest spot* in the car is the center of the rear seat.
* Make sure that the restraint meets the current government standards.
* Buy the right model for your child's size and age.
* If your car seat has a tether strap, you *must* install it properly. If you don't, your child is not safe.
* Car seats should allow your child to look out a window. Avoid the kind with the attached plastic steering wheels.

For further information about car safety, write to:

Action for Child Transportation Safety, Inc.
400 Central Park West #15P
New York, New York 10025
   Ask for the free fact sheet listing the safe car seats available today.

Physicians for Automotive Safety
50 Union Avenue
Irvington, New Jersey 17111
   Send 35¢ to receive the booklet *Don't Risk Your Child's Life*. Enclose a self-addressed, stamped, long white envelope.

Department of Transportation
National Highway Traffic Safety Administration
400 Seventh Street SW
Washington, D.C. 20590
   Send for a free pamphlet *Child Restraint Systems for Your Automobile*.

WHERE TO CHANGE BABY

I found a great place to change my baby on a car trip. Our car has a hatch-back, which when opened, provides a convenient and clean changing area. I keep a clean blanket and a favorite toy back there to make it a comfortable and happy time. Many car trunks will serve the same purpose.

Janis Woodward
Monrovia, California

In the diaper bag we stored a receiving blanket to lay the baby on while changing him in a restroom. This worked until Adam was about 9 months old. Then he preferred to be changed while standing on the back seat of the car. Never count on changing your baby in a restroom. Many are so filthy that the inconvenience of the car is far superior because it is much more sanitary.

Lisa Ginsburgh
Schaumburg, Illinois

MATTRESS PAD

We were never in a motel that provided a mattress pad for the crib. The first time. we improvised with a bath towel. Later we always travelled with our own mattress pad. Many hotels do not provide crib sheets either, so if space permits, bring several of your own.

Lisa Ginsburgh
Schaumburg, Illinois

TAKE POTTY NECESSITIES

When we went on a car trip with our 2½-year-old, we took along her potty seat and potty chair. We used the potty chair when we stopped along the road in those instances when we couldn't find a gas station. We used the potty seat in the hotel room.

Authors
Omaha, Nebraska

BABY FOOD

I feed the baby a jar of yogurt or toddler-sticks for snacks while travelling. This little nourishment allows us to get in a few hours of driving before breakfast. These foods are easy to feed the baby and there are no crumbs. We also carry a thermos of water and little cans of juice.

Lisa Ginsburgh
Schaumburg, Illinois

SNACK BAG

On long trips pack a fun snack bag or picnic basket for your toddler. My son loves to help pack the food. He looks forward to his snacks because I let him choose anything from the bag.

Include only healthy foods such as peanuts, peanut butter and graham crackers, fruits, cheese cubes, whole grain crackers, cookies (oatmeal), or carrot, minature raisin boxes, and sesame chips. Don't forget baby towelettes for easy cleaning of fingers!

Authors
Omaha, Nebraska

PEANUT BUTTER AND CHEESE SPREAD

Keep a jar of peanut butter or pressurized cheese spread in the car for emergencies. Whenever we came upon a restaurant with nothing for our son to eat, we could always request bread or crackers and make a sandwich.

Lisa Ginsburgh
Schaumburg, Illinois

BABY FOOD FLAKES

When we travelled with our baby he was 8 months old. I brought along my electric heating dish and baby food *flakes*, not the jarred kind. Since we had no refrigerator available, I mixed what I wanted with water and kept the rest sealed. Even though these were more expensive, it saved a lot of hassles.

Authors
Omaha, Nebraska

TAPE STORIES AND SONGS

Tape your child's favorite songs and stories (spoken and sung by yourself or from records) on tapes for your auto stereo. The tapes will save your voice from getting hoarse on long cross-country trips!

Lynda Halbridge
Riverside, California

MAPS AND TRAFFIC LIGHTS

On long trips, my toddler enjoys holding small maps and telling me to go "straight," "turn," or "stop" at red lights. We talk about each place we're going so he can anticipate the fun to be had at the end of the long ride. We also look at the traffic lights and he enjoys giving directions for the appropriate light color. It is an easy way to teach red, green, and yellow colors!

Authors
Omaha, Nebraska

TEACH NEW SONGS

Use the time on long trips to teach your child new nursery rhymes and songs. This can become real quality time to spend together!

Also, make up your own stories that include the child as the main character. He will enjoy the attention!

Authors
Omaha, Nebraska

USE A CAR SEAT

Use a car seat all of the time when your child is a baby and he will not balk at being tied in when he grows older. My 2½-year-old actually prefers to sit in the car seat because he can see more of the scenery.

Authors
Omaha, Nebraska

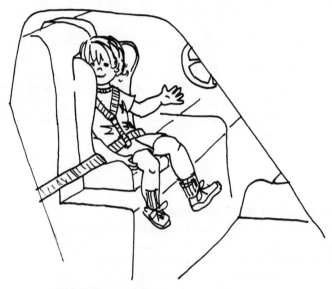

CAR SEAT TOYS

Tie small toys or teething rings to your child's car seat with a short piece of elastic. The child will have fun pulling on the elastic and the toys will always be readily available.

Authors
Omaha, Nebraska

When Leigh-Anne travels in the car seat or stroller, I tie a diaper through a teething ring or play keys. I tie the other end of the diaper to whatever she's sitting in. This way, she can play with the toy, but if she loses her grip, the diaper prevents the object from falling to the floor. The extra diaper always comes in handy anyway!

Deborah Levin-Brown
Miami Beach, Florida

CAR GAMES

When riding in the car, I bring toys and picture books for the baby. For our toddler, the car provides the opportunity for a great learning experience. We play games such as counting cars, naming the colors of cars, and pointing out different types of vehicles like a bus or a trash truck. Our older daughter likes to tell her daddy when the light turns green so we can go. We also mention right and left turns.

Mary Jane DiChiacchio
Lansdowne, Pennsylvania

HOT SEAT

In the summertime, my baby's car seat becomes very hot. I keep a few towels in the car to put on the seat when this happens.

Authors
Omaha, Nebraska

SMALL TOYS

Since Annie was 5 months old, I have tied small chewable toys to each end of the ties on the hood of her snowsuit. Wherever we go, my daughter always has something to occupy her time. Best of all, I never have to pick up toys that have been dropped from her car seat or stroller.

Karen Maizel
Lakewood, Ohio

VISUAL FUN

We always put my 2-month old, Matthew, in a car seat while travelling, but I felt he lacked visual stimulation. All he could see was the back of the seat of the car. So my husband and I found some cute pictures of animals, babies, whatever, and we taped them to the back seat of the car. We change the pictures periodically for variety. We also do this on the side of his bassinette.

Ann Louise Wolf
Newton, Massachusetts

CANVAS SUIT CASE
When travelling anywhere with my 11-month-old daughter, I carry a small canvas suitcase instead of a diaper bag. Items aren't visible in the suitcase, you can get much more inside, and it's just as easy to carry.

Inside the suitcase, I keep a small first-aid kit. I also throw in powder, pins, and bath oil, all of the items necessary for quick diaper changes.

Laura Mott
Mayfield Heights, Ohio

CLEAN-UP
Whenever we travel, I always carry a wet washcloth in a plastic bag for quick wipe-ups.

Kate Cavanaugh
Washington, D.C.

EXTRAS
Keep spare diapers and plastic bags stored in the glove compartment of your car. The plastic bags are good to hold dirty diapers in.

Gail Zweigel
Atlanta, Georgia

PACKED BAG
Get a bag that will hang on the back of a stroller. In the bag keep extra diapers, a change of baby clothing, and a blanket. This saves last minute hurrying when you need to make a quick get-away.

Donna Hatfield
Monrovia, California

GIVE YOURSELF A REST
Mothers: let your kids walk to the car and climb into their car seats, especially if you have an attached garage. We mothers do far too much lugging of toddlers who are really able to do it by themselves.

Nancy Oberst
Omaha, Nebraska

Shopping

BOTTLE HAPPINESS

Much to my surprise, I discovered that if I pushed out all of the air from the bag in a Playtex baby bottle, the suction allowed my son to drink without having to tip up the bottle. He could drink while sitting up which was especially handy when we went shopping or when we were in the car. The bottle kept him quiet and me sane!

Jennifer J. Sixt
Chesterland, Ohio

BALLOON

I've found that a bright balloon on a short string tied to the front of my baby's stroller at his head level, keeps him fascinated for a long time.

Jeannine Adams
Atlanta, Georgia

NECKLACE AMUSEMENT

When I take my daughter Andrea along to run errands I always wear a sturdy necklace. Why? The necklace gives Andrea something to play with while I am holding her. It keeps her quiet and amused while we're at the cash register, the doctor's office, wherever!

The best kind of necklace for a baby is a handmade one. Simply take a leather strand and pull through it several colorful and large beads. Be daring and add a few feathers. This necklace will keep any baby amused and you might even receive a few compliments!

Authors
Omaha, Nebraska

SHOPPING CART SAFETY

When shopping with a 1-year-old, bring a wide strip of cloth to tie the baby to the seat of the shopping cart. It prevents him from standing and falling out while you shop.

Mrs. LeRoy Ladnier
Biloxi, Mississippi

Visiting In-Town

GRANDMA'S HOUSE

Since my baby and I visit Grandma often, I keep
many items at her house, so I won't have to drag
things back and forth. She has bottles, nipples, ready-
to-feed formula, bibs, a heating dish, flake baby food,
a small spoon and disposable diapers, not to mention
many toys! Grandma also has a portable crib and a
high chair.

Authors
Omaha, Nebraska

KEEPING CHEST DRY

When I dress my baby to go out, I hate to cover
his beautiful little suits with a bib, so I put the bib
under his clothes. This way his chest stays dry,
everyone can see how beautifully he's dressed, and
he doesn't tug and pull on the bib. Obviously this hint
only works when a bib is used to catch dribbling and
not for feeding time.

Susan Guy
Chalmette, Louisianna

TRANSPORTING TOYS

When taking my 11-month-old daughter to Grandma's house, I put a few of her favorite toys in a
plastic utility bucket. The bucket is easy to carry and
also serves as a toy box for all of the little items she
wants to bring.

Laura Mott
Mayfield Heights, Ohio

IMPROVISED PACIFIER

When you are visiting someone and your child is
in desperate need of a pacifier, stuff Kleenex tightly into a nipple and the baby won't suck air.

Carol Parsow
Elkhorn, Nebraska

CUPS

When travelling or visiting friends with a baby, purchase plastic Tupperware cups with fitted covers and spouts. They save you from a lot of clean-ups. A collapsible cup is also good to use.

Gail Zweigel
Atlanta, Georgia

PORTABLE DIAPER PAD

When I'm at someone else's house, I use the pad out of my baby's infant seat as a portable diaper changing pad. This works great!

Sally Lewis
Albuquerque, New Mexico

READY FOR BED

Change your child into night clothes when you are taking him out visiting in the evening. This saves time as he will be ready to pop into bed as soon as you get home.

Joan Feldman
Cincinnati, Ohio

Dining Out

NO STRAP

If you are out to dinner with your baby and the restaurant's highchair is missing straps, use your husband's belt. It works great in a pinch. You can also use this idea if a rented stroller is strapless.

Donna Hersch
Omaha, Nebraska

FEED AT HOME

When you are going out to eat lunch or dinner, feed the children something before leaving home. If they're hungry, they can get very crabby and wild. If they're full when dinner arrives, give them "fussy" food to nibble on. Peas or french fries will do nicely.

Jennifer J. Sixt
Chesterland, Ohio

PAPER PLATES

Whenever I go to a restaurant with my toddler,
I bring paper plates along. He eats on them without
any problems. This avoids his eating on a dirty
highchair tray.

Lynda Halbridge
Riverside, California

FUN BAG

I have four children, ages 6 and under, and my husband and I occasionally like to take the kids out to
dinner. I always bring along my bag of tricks to make
sure their restaurant manners don't falter. The bag
includes Cheerios, crackers, pieces of cheese, fruit,
small toys, books, and puzzles. I bring out goodies
one at a time and they help keep the meal peaceful
and quiet for all.

Deborah Gans
Goleta, California

RESTLESS CHILD

My toddler was difficult to take to a restaurant
because he wouldn't sit still for a very long time in
the high chair. So now we do one of two things.
Either we order and then walk around with him
before our food comes, or we call to order ahead of
time so our food will be ready when we get there.

Authors
Omaha, Nebraska

TOWEL

If we ever eat in anyone's house with our
youngster, I always ask for a large towel to put
under his highchair. This way I don't have to worry
that he will spill food on their carpet.

Authors
Omaha, Nebraska

Avoiding
Accidents

Children suffer many hurts as they grow and mothers are helpless to shield them. Your baby will tumble while attempting to walk. An overly loving sister or brother will make a hug feel more like strangulation. A toddler will scrape his knees raw before he conquers the swingset. Life is full of such obstacles, but your child shouldn't have to confront hazards that you *can* do something about.

Picture the following common household scenes. A bottle of medicine is left forgotten on the dressing table. An iron stands on the ironing board long after the clothes are pressed. A beautiful Pointsettia adorns a coffee table. A sheet of plastic wraps newly dry-cleaned dresses in a closet. A shiny penny lies wedged in the carpet within Baby's view. None of these situations is out of the ordinary. Yet all are potentially deadly to your child.

Accidents happen, but they don't have to. Most can be prevented by taking simple steps to safeguard your house for children. This chapter will aid you in taking these very important precautionary measures. However, if the worst does happen, you need to know how to react using the basic first aid techniques we have included. Watchful, loving eyes and the following information will make your house a safer place for you and your family.

Indoors 91

The Kitchen 94

The Bathroom 96

The Bedroom 98

Other Areas 100

First Aid 103

PRIME TIME FOR AN ACCIDENT TO HAPPEN

When Mom

* is fixing dinner
* is sick, pregnant or extremely tired
* is rushed

When Mom and Dad

* are arguing
* have a lot of outside pressures and stresses
* are out and someone else is caring for your child

When Children

* are rushed
* are very tired
* are extremely thirsty or hungry
* are up in early morning before parents are up

When the Family

* is moving
* is on a trip

Indoors

SAFEGUARD THE HOUSE

Stores carry many safety devices to help avoid accidents in the home. Buy locks for cabinet doors, gates for the tops and bottoms of the stairs, and plastic plugs to be inserted in electrical outlets. These inexpensive devices will save you a lot of worry.

Authors
Omaha, Nebraska

POISONS

We avoid accident in our home by putting all of the poisons in one cabinet. We put a clasp and lock on it, and we hide the keys.

Mrs. Dawn Skinner
East Hartford, Connecticut

BELLS ON SHOES

The best way to avoid accidents is to know where your children are at all times. I put bells on my children's shoes so I can hear where they are in the house without having to watch them every second.

Sally Lewis
Albuquerque, New Mexico

HOUSEHOLD CONTAINERS

When giving your baby or toddler household containers for playtime, be selective. Never use brittle plastic, metal-edged containers, or anything that once held any form of medicine, cosmetic or soap. Your child might find a full bottle sometime and not distinguish it from his own playthings.

Authors
Omaha, Nebraska

FIRE SAFETY

* Use caution if you smoke. Don't smoke in bed or while carrying Baby. Also, don't leave cigarettes around for Baby to eat.

* Have fire extinguishers on every floor of your house, including the kitchen.

* Use a safety screen in front of your fireplace and guards in front of the radiators.

* Never leave matches or cigarette lighters lying around the house.

* Install smoke detectors in your home, at least one on every floor. Test them regularly.

* Teach your child early to stay away from things that will burn: stove, hot drinks, lit candles, matches and burning cigarettes.

* Teach your youngster what to do in a fire emergency. Show the older children how to help the babies. Practice the escape routes with them, using at least two routes in case one is locked.

* Buy flame-resistant clothing for your child.

* Buy a fire ladder and store it near your bedroom window.

* Turn Christmas lights off at night.

PLANTS

Be selective in the kinds of plants you keep in the house. Many common household plants, such as the Philodendron, are poisonous! If in doubt, put them out of Baby's reach or better yet give them to a childless friend!

Inez Davis
Kansas City, Missouri

Teach your child to leave plants alone. The following plants are poisonous when eaten. If your child swallows *any* part of the plant, call your Poison Control Center immmediately.

Amaryllis	Azalea
Baneberry	Bittersweet
Black Locust	Bleeding Heart
Castor Bean	Christmas Rose
Daffodil	Daphne
Dieffenbacia	English Ivy
Foxglove	Holly
Hyacinth	Lily-of-the-Valley
Mistletoe	Morning Glory
Philodendron	Poison Hemlock
Poinsettia	Pokeweed
Privet	Tomato Leaves
Rhubarb Leaves	Water Hemlock
Wisteria	Yew

The Kitchen

KEEP BABY OUT

Avoid accidents by keeping your baby out of the kitchen or at least on the opposite end of the room when cooking. Also, it's a good idea to cook on the back burners of the stove, especially if your child can reach up.

Inez Davis
Kansas City, Missouri

VERBALIZE THE DANGERS

Let your child get a close-up view of the mixer, iron, knife, and other potentially dangerous kitchen items. Explain how they work and point out the dangers involved with each. Be sure he understands that only adults can use these pieces of equipment. Often this will be enough to curb the child's curiosity.

Helen Cain
Omaha, Nebraska

PREVENTING CHOKING

I've always been afraid that my children will choke on their food, so I made a rule in our house: no eating food unless they are sitting down. I've heard that children can choke while walking and eating things like carrots or celery sticks. I'm always in the same room while they're eating. Also, when my children were just starting to eat finger foods, I was very careful to cut up the food into tiny pieces.

Authors
Omaha, Nebraska

BEWARE OF HOT FOOD

One time I saw a mother drink coffee while holding her baby on her lap. It didn't take long for that baby to grab the coffee and spill it all over herself and her mom. So now whenever we have any hot food or hot drink at home, I don't hold my child and I move the hot items to the center of the table.

Authors
Omaha, Nebraska

KITCHEN SAFETY

★ ★ Most childhood accidents that occur in the home take place in the kitchen.

* Keep knives and other sharp utensils locked away.

* Use the back burners whenever possible. Pot handles should be turned towards the rear of the stove.

* Don't use an electrical appliance near water. When you're finished using it, keep it out of reach of children.

* Unplug small appliances when not in use.

* Keep the high chair and playpen far away from your work area.

* Hanging tablecloths should be avoided.

* Don't allow running in the kitchen.

* Make sure your kitchen floor is not slippery. When you spill something, wipe it up immediately.

* Keep ant and roach traps out of your child's reach.

* Always fasten the strap on your baby's highchair.

* While you're cooking a meal, don't let Baby crawl around in the kitchen.

* If you have sliding glass doors, put colored decals on them.

* Do not leave a partially filled mop bucket on the floor.

* Every kitchen should have a chemical fire extinguisher. Know how to use it and keep it out of the reach of children.

POP BOTTLES

I had a friend whose baby was injured when a pop bottle exploded. Now we keep all of our soda drinks locked up in a cabinet.

Authors
Omaha, Nebraska

TRASH HIDDEN

It's very important to keep trash sacks and cans out of a child's reach. We throw many dangerous things in our trash, so we keep the can secured.

Authors
Omaha, Nebraska

The Bathroom

BATHROOM SAFETY

The bathroom is the second most dangerous area in the house.

* Test the tub temperature before putting your child in.

* Never leave your baby or young child unattended in the bathtub.

* Don't let your child use any electrical appliance around water.

* Put a lock on your medicine cabinet. Also lock up your toiletries.

* Place rubber, non-skid mats or flowers inside your tub and shower. (Mats are preferable)

* Always keep your bathroom door closed.

* Leave the door lock off so he won't lock himself in.

* Beware of toilet lids falling on Baby's hands and heads.

* Emphasize to your child that he should not turn on the hot water, nor should he stand up in the bathtub.

* Avoid slippery floors. Teach "no running" in the bathroom.

RED FOR HOT

I always worried about my 2-year-old turning on the hot water faucet in the bathtub and burning herself. I solved the problem by using a marker pen to put a red dot on the hot faucet. She now knows not to turn this one on.

Authors
Omaha, Nebraska

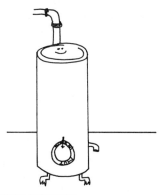

AVOIDING BURNS

Turn your water heater thermostat to below scalding. You never want the water to come out so scalding hot that it will burn Baby's soft skin.

Inez Davis
Kansas City, Missouri

NO GLASS CUPS

I used a glass drinking cup in our bathroom because it matched the decor. One night my daughter dropped it in the sink, I learned my lesson and now use paper or plastic drinking cups.

Authors
Omaha, Nebraska

NO LOCK ON DOOR

When we first moved into our house, we noticed that the lock on our bathroom door could not be opened from the outside. Since we had heard of young children locking themselves in bathrooms, we had the entire lock unit replaced.

Authors
Omaha, Nebraska

The Bedroom

USE FLOOR

One day I left my 3-month-old in the middle of our
big bed for a moment while I walked into the
hallway. When I came back in the room, he had
scooted all the way to the edge and in another 10
seconds would have fallen off. I learned my lesson
and now put him on the floor if I have to go into
another room.

Authors
Omaha, Nebraska

CLIMBING OUT OF CRIB

There comes a time when your baby will probably
start to climb out of the crib. The fall could hurt him.
Often a lack of space or tight finances won't permit
purchasing a youth bed at this time. Since the child
is going to climb over the top anyway, lower the mattress as close to the floor as possible and lower the
side rail. The rail will still prevent your child from
rolling out while sleeping, but when he tries to climb
out he will have a shorter distance to fall. Putting
a stool or big soft pillows on the floor helps too. This
way you can use the crib longer.

Keren Garcia
Monrovia, California

PLASTIC BAGS

When we get clothes back from the cleaners, I
never allow the plastic bags to hang in the bedroom
closet. I always throw the bags away. I tie the bag
in knots before putting it into the wastebasket.

Lynda Halbridge
Riverside, California

FLAME RETARDANT CLOTHING

All sleepwear that I buy for my children is labeled "flame retardant." When it's Halloween time, I
avoid buying costumes made of disposable paper. It
is a fire hazard.

Authors
Omaha, Nebraska

LOOSE THREADS

Whenever you buy baby clothing (especially sleepers), always check for any loose hanging threads. One time, my baby got a very sore toe when a thread twisted around it.

Authors
Omaha, Nebraska

LOOSE BUTTONS

I used to worry that my baby's buttons would fall off his clothes and he would swallow one. Now I reinforce all of the buttons before he wears his outfit.

Authors
Omaha, Nebraska

SCREEN DOOR

I use a screen door with a latch hook lock in my toddler's room. My husband added the screen door when Ginger began to walk and could climb out of her crib. If she should get out of bed I can see and hear her through the door and she can't get hurt by going near the stairs or by getting into something she shouldn't.

Mrs. Virginia Fallon
Turnersville, New Jersey

BEDROOM SAFETY

* Nursery equipment should be well-constructed and safe, and painted with lead-free paint.
* Make sure all of your windows and screens are secure.
* Don't put pillows, small objects or large toys in crib. He could use them to climb out.
* Always close diaper pins when not in use, and store away from Baby's reach.
* Never leave your baby alone on a bed or changing table.
* Don't use insect repellent strips in nursery.
* Never place the crib under a window.
* Don't use bunk beds for young children.

Other Areas

DINING ROOM TABLE

With a 4-year-old, 2-year-old, and a 9-month-old in the house, it's an all day affair keeping curious fingers out of where they don't belong. I keep a tablecloth on my dining room table and my children have discovered the trick of pulling one corner and clearing the table in one swoop. I solved the problem by stitching wide elastic strips underneath each corner and taping it to the leaves of the table. We now avoid breaking dishes and little heads don't have things falling on them.

Kathi Gillette
Rockford, Illinois

SHARP CORNERS

When my child David was learning to stand, I made safeguards for the corners of our coffee table. I found some old styrofoam, cut it to the right size and taped it to the four corners with masking tape. Now I don't have to worry about him hitting his head on a sharp corner.

Lynda Halbridge
Riverside, California

SHUT DOOR TO LAUNDRY ROOM

I always shut my laundry room door. Would you believe my little one opened the dryer door and climbed in?

Patty Nogg
Council Bluffs, Iowa

GARAGE HAZARDS

The garage can be a very dangerous place for children. My husband eliminated some of the potential hazards by building storage shelves up high to store dangerous items. We used to store empty pop bottles on the garage floor. One time our son played with them, dropped a bottle and cut himself. Now we put bottles up there also.

Authors
Omaha, Nebraska

STAIR SAFETY

* Use safety glass at the bottom and top of the stairs.

* Teach your baby to crawl backwards down the steps.

* If your child is just beginning to walk up and down steps, walk behind him when he's going up, and in front of him when he's going down.

* Have your child use the handrail whenever he goes up or down the steps.

* Carpet the steps, if possible.

* Put a night light in the hallway by the steps in case your child wanders out of his room at night.

* There should be no running or playing on the steps.

* Place no toys or other objects on stairs.

FAMILY ROOM SAFETY

* All tables with sharp corners should have some type of protective covering on the corners.

* Be aware of hanging cords on tables.

* Store breakable objects up high, not on tables.

* Throw away cigarette butts at once.

* Keep fireplace screened at all times. Fireplace crystals are poisonous.

GARAGE OR BASEMENT SAFETY

* The safest thing to do is to lock these areas.

* If you're storing freezers and refrigerators, remove the doors.

* All tools should be locked up.

* *Always* disconnect power tools when they're not in use.

MEMORIZE INFO
We taught our son his phone number and street
address when he was 3½. It took quite awhile for
him to learn this information, but we think it is very
important if he should ever get lost.
Authors
Omaha, Nebraska

OUTSIDE SAFETY

* If possible, fence your child's play yard, or use a playpen.

* Always keep an eye on your child's outside activities.

* Avoid playing around the street or driveway.

* Check for holes in your yard. They should be filled.

* All unused swimming pools should be drained or covered up.

* If your child uses a small pool, don't leave water in it.

* Don't allow playing in yard if grass and shrubs have been sprayed.

HOLD HANDS
My daughter, Andrea, 2½, always holds my hand
in a parking lot. It's been a rule since she was little.
She also knows not to cross any streets without my
assistance (although I always expect the unexpected).
Authors
Omaha, Nebraska

EMERGENCY NUMBERS
I always keep a list of emergency numbers next
to *each* phone, because you never know where you
will be or what you will forget when you are in a
state of panic.
Authors
Omaha, Nebraska

First Aid

BASIC PROCEDURES

On the inside of a kitchen cupboard door, I've taped a sheet of paper with some simple first-aid procedures on it. This list is in a very accessible spot.

Authors
Omaha, Nebraska

SPLINTER

My mom had an old trick to get a splinter out when we were little. She would numb the splinter area with an ice cube before she tried to remove it.

Authors
Omaha, Nebraska

BUMPS

We all know how often toddlers fall and bump their heads! Put rubbing alcohol on the bump right away and they won't get a bruise. If you don't have rubbing alcohol, try vinegar.

Therese Sorum
Omaha, Nebraska

RECOMMENDED FIRST AID BOOKS

CHILD SAFETY IS NO ACCIDENT, A PARENTS HANDBOOK OF EMERGENCIES by Jay M. Arena, M.D. and Miriam Bachar, M.S. (Duke University Press)

A SIGH OF RELIEF-THE FIRST-AID HANDBOOK FOR CHILDHOOD EMERGENCIES produced by Martin I. Green (Bantam Books)

BAND-AID BLISS

My 4-year-old used to get very upset when I'd try to remove his band-aid. I discovered that if you rub a little baby oil over the area (only a perforated band-aid works), you can make the removal truly painless.

Authors
Omaha, Nebraska

POPSICLES

Always keep popsicles in the freezer for Baby's hurts, especially cuts in the mouth. The popsicle will stop the bleeding faster and better than a cold cloth.

Linda Larson
Troy, New York

BLEEDING CUTS (Minor)

1. Control the bleeding by pressing the wound with gauze or a clean cloth.

2. When the bleeding stops, pour a large amount of hydrogen peroxide over the injury. It loosens the dirt particles.

3. Wash the skin area around the wound with mild soap and rinse under running water.

SEVERE BLEEDING

1. CALL FOR HELP IMMEDIATELY.

2. Apply direct pressure at once with a clean cloth, gauze or the cleanest clothing item around. Continue pressing on the wound until bleeding stops or help arrives.

3. Elevate the injured part unless there is a broken bone.

4. If the original dressing becomes soaked with blood, don't remove it, just add more dressing on top and continue pressure.

5. If you have no material to use for the dressing, use your hand to press on the wound.

6. After the bleeding stops, bandage the wound snugly.

7. Observe for signs of SHOCK, (see page 110).

ALSO CALL YOUR DOCTOR WHEN:

*   An object is lodged in the skin. (Don't try to remove it.)

*   Direct pressure does not stop the bleeding.

*   Your child is bleeding from an animal or human bite.

*   There is a face or wrist cut.

*   You have any questions at all.

BREATHING: ARTIFICIAL RESPIRATION

CALL FOR HELP IMMEDIATELY

Check for breathing. If child *is not* breathing:

1. With your finger, remove any particles in the child's mouth.

2. Place the child on his back, put your hand under his neck and tip his head back. Chin should point upward. This opens the air passage.

3. Listen for any breathing and look for the chest to rise and fall.

   If breathing *does not* occur:

   a) Put your mouth over the child's *mouth and nose*, making a leakproof seal. Puff 4 small, gentle breaths. Watch to see if the chest rises.

   b) Repeat every 3 seconds, using short, gentle puffs of air. After each breath, take your mouth away and listen for air coming out.

   c) Continue until the child breathes on his own.

   d) If the child does not start breathing by himself, see CHOKING, page 107. Then begin ARTIFICIAL RESPIRATION at point #1 again. Continue until the child breathes on his own, or until help comes.

NOTE: If your child vomits, tilt his head to the side, clear away any vomit that might be blocking his throat, and continue.

BUMPS

1. Apply ice bag or cold compress right after the injury. This will reduce the swelling.

MINOR BURNS AND SUNBURNS

First Degree Burns: Reddening of the skin.
Second Degree Burns: Blistering of the skin.

1. Submerge the burned skin in cold water immediately, until the pain is gone. Don't apply grease.

2. Blot dry with a clean cloth.

3. Cover the burned area loosely with a dry gauze bandage.

4. Don't apply creams or oils of any kind (sprays, butter, etc.) to burns.

5. Leave the blisters alone. Don't pop them.

SERIOUS BURNS

Third Degree Burns: White, charred or broken skin. Child feels little pain.

1. CALL FOR MEDICAL HELP IMMEDIATELY.

2. Keep yourself and your child calm.

3. Don't apply anything to the burned area.

4. Don't give him anything to drink.

5. Don't touch burn.

6. Cover burned area lightly with a *dry* clean sheet, cloth or gauze bandage.

7. Elevate the burned area, if possible.

8. Treat for shock, if necessary. (see SHOCK, page 110)

CHOKING

Let the child cough the object up, if he can.

If your child *cannot* breathe, cough, cry, or speak:

1. Place your infant or young child on his stomach, head down over your knees or forearm. Give four sharp, crisp blows between the shoulder blades with the *heel* of your hand.

2. If the object is not dislodged, do the Heimlich maneuver:

   Stand behind your child with the thumbside of your fist between his navel and the rib cage. Cover your fist with your other hand. Let his upper body hang forward. Thrust upward and inward rapidly several times until the object pops out.

3. If the object comes out but your child has difficulty in breathing, he may require artificial respiration. (see BREATHING: ARTIFICIAL RESPIRATION, page 105)

For a free card telling about the Heimlich Manuever, send a stamped, self-addressed, long envelope to:

The Health Education Department
Blue Cross and Blue Shield of Massachusetts
P.O. Box 1178
Boston, Massachusetts 02103

POISON

TO AVOID A POISONING ACCIDENT

* Keep all of your dangerous products out of reach of children.

* Put child-proof locks on *all* cupboards which contain medicines or other harmful products.

* Use child-proof caps on all medicines and bottles.

* As soon as your child is old enough to understand, explain the dangers of poison.

* Don't put poisonous substances in food or beverage containers.

* Don't store harmful products on the same shelves with food.

* When using paints, make sure your baby or small child does not inhale the toxic fumes.

POISONS TO KEEP OUT OF A CHILD'S REACH

If your child swallows any of the following materials call the *Poison Control Center* immediately.

Parent's Bedroom

Birth control pills
Cigarettes and matches
Contraceptive creams
Plants
Shoe polish
Sleeping pills, other drugs

Kitchen

Ammonia
Candles
Copper cleaner
Dishwasher detergents
Drain cleaners
Floor cleaners
Furniture polish
Glue
Medicines
Oven cleaners
Soaps
Vitamin pills

Laundry Room

Bleaches
Detergents
Dyes
Rug Shampoo
Soaps

Bathroom

Aerosol sprays
All drugs and pills
Aspirin
Astringents
Bubble bath
Deodorants
Drain cleaners
Hair rinses
Hair sprays
Laxatives
Lotions
Mouthwash
Nail polish remover
Perfume
Shampoo
Toilet bowl cleaner

Garage or Basement

Anti-freeze
Charcoal starter
Fertilizer
Gasoline
Insecticides
Mothballs
Paints
Paint remover
Paint thinner
Plant food
Turpentine

When giving medicines:

*   Don't ever refer to medicine as candy.

*   Read the instructions on the medicine bottle at least two times before giving it to anyone. Never give it in the the dark.

*   Don't refill a prescription unless you consult your doctor.

*   Throw away medicine that is too old.

Poison Aid ™ Emergency Poison Treatment and Prevention System includes:

— ipecac syrup

— activated charcoal

— six warning labels

— question and answer pamphlet

— wall chart that has steps on what to do when there has been a suspected poisoning.

available at some major drugstores or write to:

PBS Medical Systems, Inc.
P.O. Box 89
Summit, New Jersey 07901

Write to receive free pamphlet *Preventing Childhood Poisionings*:

Food & Drug Administration
Office of Consumer Affairs
Consumer Communications Staff
5600 Fishers Lane
Rockville, Maryland 20857

SCRAPES (The skinned knee type)

1. If debris is not removed from the skin, an infection could develop. Wash at once with soap and water.

2. Apply hydrogen peroxide on wound.

3. Cover with one layer of sterile gauze (make sure it does not stick)

4. Watch the cut closely for possible infection.

SHOCK

A severely injured child must be treated for shock.

Shock Signs: Cold and clammy skin, pale face, weak pulse, shallow
     breathing, nausea or vomiting, eyes may look lifeless.

1. Until help arrives, lay him down, face up and loosely cover with *one*
    blanket. If he has no broken bones, elevate legs.

2. Stay next to your child and reassure him. Do *not* give him food or
    water, no matter how much he may want it.

3. CALL FOR AN AMBULANCE IMMEDIATELY.

SPLINTERS

1. Using soap and water wash the child's skin around the splinter.

2. Loosen the skin with a sterile needle and take out the splinter with
    tweezers. Gently squeeze the skin.

3. Apply rubbing alcohol and cover with a sterile bandage.

SPRAINS

1. Calm your child, and elevate the sprained joint to reduce swelling.
    (For ankle sprain, have him lie down and put pillows under his ankle
    and leg.)

2. Keep an ice bag or *cold* compress on the sprain.

3. Call your doctor. If pain continues your child should be examined.

Illness

Some mothers could find the doctor's office if they had to drive there blind-folded. You'll discover that the path will be imbedded in your memory just from the routine visits alone, not counting the additional trips when your child is sick.

At times, you may feel as though you live at the doctor's office and only go home for visits. First-time mothers are especially prone to camping in waiting rooms. They may rush in with Baby's first runny nose "emergency" and panic when diaper rash invades Baby's bottom.

Eventually moms learn to handle many situations on their own and can better judge when the doctor's help is needed. In those cases, nothing beats the pediatrician's reassuring voice when at 3 A.M. a sick child has taken a sudden turn for the worse. It's comforting for parents to realize they do not have to handle medical emergencies alone. A professional's help can be just a phone call away. It's not surprising that some women speak very affectionately about Baby's doctor.

Learning to be adept with a rectal thermometer is not one of motherhood's most glamourous moments. Yet it's an inevitable part of the job. Eventually your nursing skills will become second nature. You won't panic when a cold, the flu, or even the measles invade your house. So take the time to look over the following problems your child may face. The information will help you handle whatever the future brings with a larger measure of confidence.

Visits to the Doctor....................113

A Sick Child.........................119

Visits To The Doctor

PREPARING FOR THE VISIT
I bought my toddler a doctor's kit and taught her what each object is used for. Now she seems more comfortable when she sees the pediatrician.

Gail Furman
Springfield, Virginia

Right before we go to the doctor's office, I always dress my baby in clothes that are easy to take off and put back on. It saves time and a hassle when a child may be a little upset. We also use throw-away diapers to make the trip easier.

Authors
Omaha, Nebraska

DENTIST
We began to prepare my toddler for her first visit to the dentist about two weeks in advance. We discussed her teeth, the chair she would sit in, and the instruments the dentist would use.
Then we played "dentist." I would be the dentist and look in her mouth and then it would be her turn to play the role of dentist. The result of this advanced preparation was that my little girl was not afraid when she made her first visit.

Pam Wilczek
Chicago, Illinois

BOOKS TO READ TO YOUNGSTER BEFORE VISITING DOCTOR, DENTIST OR GOING TO THE HOSPITAL

- *Nurse Nancy* by Kathryn Jackson (Golden Press)
- *Nicky Goes To The Doctor* by Richard Scarry (Golden Press)
- *Bugs Bunny Visits The Dentist* by Seyour Reit (Golden Press)
- *My Friend The Dentist* by Jane Werner Watson, Robert E. Switzer, M.D. & J. Cotter Hirschberg, M.D. (Golden Press)
- *My Friend The Doctor* by Jane Werner Watson, Robert E. Switzer, M.D. & J. Cotter Hirschberg, M.D. (Golden Press)
- *Curious George Goes To The Hospital* by Margaret & H.A. Rey (Houghton Mifflin)

COMMON AILMENTS OF YOUNG CHILDREN

AILMENT	DESCRIPTION	TREATMENT
Colds	Child may sneeze, cough, have a sore throat. May have runny or stuffed nose. Possible low fever.	Clear Baby's nose with nasal syringe. Use a coolmist humidifier for easier breathing. Take child to doctor if he has a deep, persistent or wheezing cough (without fever). Call doctor if he has a fever of 101° or more. Avoid chilling. Keep room warm (around 72°).
Constipation	Child is not able to have bowel movement for 3-4 days, or stools are very hard and become difficult to pass.	Call your doctor. Sometimes bottle-fed babies become constipated.
Croup (Laryngitis)	The "cold" is in the child's vocal cords. 1. *Spasmodic Croup without Fever:* Most common type. Child will have loud, barking cough. Hoarseness. Difficulty in breathing. Struggles for his breath. Usually comes at night. Attacks last from about ½-2 hours. Might have two attacks in one night. Can recur for the next two nights. 2. *Croup with Fever:* More severe type. Chest cold, along with fever and hoarseness and tight breathing. Can start slowly or quickly, any time of the day or night.	*Croup without fever:* CALL YOUR DOCTOR IMMEDIATELY. Take your child into bathroom, close the door and run a hot shower to create moist air (use tub if you don't have shower, but don't put him in the tub). Let him inhale the steam. STAY WITH YOUR CHILD. Important to keep his bedroom moist with a cold-mist humidifier. Adult should sleep in child's room for three nights. *Croup with Fever:* This is VERY SERIOUS and you should CALL YOUR DOCTOR WITHOUT DELAY. If you can't get him, take child to the nearest hospital.

Diarrhea	Bowel movements are extremely loose and more frequent than usual. The color and odor change also. Baby might have a mild intestinal infection. It is a SEVERE infection if your baby has any of these symptoms: blood or pus in the stools, watery stools, fever of 101° or more, vomiting, "sunken" eyes with dark circles under them.	Mild diarrhea in Baby: CALL YOUR DOCTOR at once to prevent dehydration.

Mild diarrhea in Children: Discontinue the usual foods. Give clear fluids such as: weak tea with sugar, 7-up, water, jello water, clear broth, gingerale, Gator Aid, crackers or toast, etc. for 24 hours. DON'T give milk. Stop medicines unless your doctor tells you otherwise.

SEVERE DIARRHEA: If your baby or young child has any of the symptoms listed to the left under SEVERE infection, you must CALL YOUR DOCTOR IMMEDIATELY. If you can't, TAKE YOUR CHILD TO A HOSPITAL. |
Ear Infections	Usually caused by colds or viral infection. Might have fever. Baby may tug or rub his ear, or cry loudly for hours.	CALL YOUR DOCTOR PROMPTLY. Medications used are more effective in the early stages of ear infections. Be sure and tell him if your child has a fever.
Prickly Heat	Mild skin rash caused by over dressing of baby in hot weather. Clusters of small pink pimples. Can develop blisters. First begins around the neck.	Keep baby's skin cool. Dust lightly with cornstarch or powder. Lightly dress or take off Baby's clothes. Call pediatrician if rash isn't gone in a few days.
Thrush (White Mouth)	A fungus infection in Baby's mouth. Looks like patches of white spots stuck on the inside of the mouth (cheeks, tongue, roof of mouth, throat). If try to wipe it off, the skin underneath will bleed slightly. Baby's mouth is sore and the pain interferes with Baby's breast-feeding.	CALL YOUR DOCTOR IMMEDIATELY. To prevent thrush, scrub and sterilize bottles and nipples.

THE FIRST SET OF TEETH

	AVERAGE AGE OF ERUPTION
UPPER	
CENTRAL INCISOR	7½-8 months
LATERAL INCISOR	9-10 months
CUSPID	18-20 months
FIRST MOLAR	14-15 months
SECOND MOLAR	24 months
LOWER	
SECOND MOLAR	20 months
FIRST MOLAR	12 months
CUSPID	16 months
LATERAL INCISOR	7-8 months
CENTRAL INCISOR	6 months

FIRST APPOINTMENT
When taking my son for his periodic check-up, I always ask for the first appointment of the day. I avoid the long wait when the doctor has gotten behind.

Linda Vogel
Omaha, Nebraska

IN THE WAITING ROOM
Whenever I suspect that there may be a long wait at the doctor's office, I pack a small picnic to keep the kids occupied. I put some ice water in a Tupperware cup with a lid and make a cheese sandwich. I give each kid one-half of the sandwich and they love their picnic! Bringing along some toys is also a help in passing the time.

Deborah Sawyer
Dracut, Maryland

Carry an old wallet with outdated credit cards, an old set of keys, and pictures, so if you have to wait in the doctor's office, your baby is occupied. This also comes in handy if you unexpectedly have to wait anywhere!

Gail Zweigel
Atlanta, Georgia

When I go to the doctor's office with my child, I take along a small pad of paper that will easily fit into my handbag along with a crayon or pencil. If there is a wait, my child can draw and keep himself busy.

Donna Short
Omaha, Nebraska

BE HONEST
When you go to see the doctor, be honest with your child! I suggest that you say: "This shot will hurt, but the doctor is giving it to you because she cares about you and wants you to stay healthy!"

Jeannine Adams
Atlanta, Georgia

SAVE SOME MONEY

If your little one needs a prescription, don't be afraid to ask your pediatrician if he has any sample drugs. Our doctor was very happy to give us some. He also told us of a pharmacy with low prices not too far from our house.

Authors
Omaha, Nebraska

SECOND OPINION

If you are not thoroughly happy with your doctor's analysis of your Baby's illness, do not hesitate to get a second opinion. It will give you peace of mind.

Authors
Omaha, Nebraska

**IT'S TIME TO CALL THE DOCTOR...
EVEN WAKE HIM UP...WHEN:**

* Your child has been in any bad accident.

* He loses consciousness or has a convulsion.

* Your sick child's condition takes a sudden turn for the worse.

* You can't stop the bleeding by using direct pressure.

* There is blood in the bowel movements.

* A fever (102° or above) won't go down after your child has taken aspirin.

* He has a negative reaction to the medication he's taking.

* Your child suffers intense abdominal pain lasting for more than ½ hour, or has severe chest pain.

* He is having trouble breathing.

* He is vomiting or has diarrhea lasting more than 2 hours.

* There is a suspected or real poisoning.

* You think your child is seriously sick and you are frightened by the way he is acting. Trust your intuition!

A Sick Child

GIVING MEDICINE

The easiest way to get liquid medicine into a baby or small child is by using a syringe, not a spoon. You can also try a vitamin dropper.

Barb Wadleigh
Madison, Wisconsin

When giving medicine to a small baby, mix it with a little juice and let the baby drink it from a bottle.

Carol Parsow
Elkhorn, Nebraska

DID YOU KNOW that you should never use your silverware teaspoon when giving medicine to your child? These teaspoons vary so much in size that you could be giving your child too much or too little. Instead, use a measuring spoon or another accurate device such as a medicine dropper.

POPSICLES

Popsicles make the perfect food for kids who are sick and need more fluids. By sucking on the popsicle they get at least two ounces of liquid.

Mothers from New London
New London, New Hampshire

HOMEMADE REMEDY

Try my homemade cough medicine. Mix some honey with lemon juice. This works well for children over one year old.

Authors
Omaha, Nebraska

SUPPLIES FOR YOUR MEDICINE CHEST

Absorbent Cotton
*Adhesive Bandages
*Adhesive Tape
Baking Soda
Butterfly Bandages
Calomine Lotion—
    to relieve itching
*Children's Aspirin—
    ask your doctor what kind
Cotton Tipped Swabs—
    to apply ointment
Cough Medicine—
    ask your doctor what kind
Hydrogen Peroxide—
    cleans wounds
Ice Bag and hot-water bottle
*Rubbing Alcohol
7-up or Ginger Ale—
    for upset stomachs
Sterile Eye Pads
*Sterile Gauze Bandages—
    2'' wide
Sterile Gauze Squares—
    3'' square in separate envelopes
*Thermometer—
    oral and rectal
*First-Aid Manual—
    contact your local Red Cross
    chapter to locate a good one

FOR BABY

*Baby Scissors
*Cold-mist vaporizer
Diaper Rash Ointment
Nasal Syringe—removes
    mucus from Baby's nose
Petroleum Jelly—helps
    with insertion of rectal
    thermometer

*Keep these starred items in
a first-aid kit. Take it travelling with you. (But keep it out
of your child's reach.)

In case of **POISONING,** you need to have the following three items:

SYRUP OF IPECAC

ACTIVATED CHARCOAL

EPSOM SALTS

USE ONLY AS DIRECTED BY YOUR POISON CONTROL CENTER OR YOUR DOCTOR. ALSO SEE PAGES 108 & 109.

SEE WHAT'S ON HAND

Before I call the doctor when Dusty is ill, I look to see what medicines I have on hand. Sometimes I don't need a new prescription which saves money.
Authors
Omaha, Nebraska

THROW OUT THE OLD

I go through our medicine chest periodically and throw out any medicines with an expired date. This way I eliminate the possibility of giving old medicines to my children.
Authors
Omaha, Nebraska

WHEN YOUR CHILD IS SICK

DO GIVE HIM   *DON'T*

* A lot of fluids: water
  and juice especially.

* Allow visitors

* Take him outside, or to
  sitter's house.

* a lot of loving, time and
  attention.

* Force him to eat if he
  doesn't want to.

* fun toys, new books, quiet
  things he can do in bed

TREATMENT FOR VOMITING

1. Immediately stop feedings.

2. Nothing to eat for 1-2 hours to give the stomach a complete rest.

3. If the child has not vomited for 2-3 hours, *small* sips of any of the following may be given:
   a. Water
   b. Cold carbonated drinks
   c. Clear liquids
   d. Clear broth soups
   e. Cold tea
   f. Fruit juices (no citrus juices)
   g. Jello

4. AVOID fatty, fried or greasy foods for the next 48 hours.

HOW TO TREAT FEVERS IN CHILDREN

1. Place child in coolest room of the house.

2. Undress child or keep clothes to a minimum.

3. Use a cool air vaporizer.

4. Encourage child to drink clear fluids such as tea, juice, water, jello water, broth or popsicles.

5. Aspirin or acetominophen (Liquiprin, Tylenol, Tempra, Prompt) may be used as your doctor suggests.

6. Sponge bathing may be used if the temperature goes beyond 103° or 104°. Place child in a tub of lukewarm water. It's too cool if your child shivers. Try to keep child in the tub for 20-45 minutes, splashing water on him. If child gets upset, you can get into the tub with him.

A high temperature may cause a child to have a FEBRILE CONVULSION. If your child has a seizure, take these steps:

1. From the area, remove any objects that might hurt him.

2. Loosen his clothing, but DON'T restrain him.

3. When seizure is over, turn the child onto his left side.

4. Check to see he is breathing well.

5. CALL THE DOCTOR AT ONCE.

THREE WAYS TO TAKE A CHILD'S TEMPERATURE

Method	Type of Thermometer	Time Needed For Accurate Reading	Recommendations
By Rectum	Rectal thermometer (has round bulb on the end)	1 minute	Best method for children under one year. Averages about one degree higher than oral temperature.
By Armpit (axilla)	Use oral or rectal thermometer. Place bulb high in child's bare armpit, then lower arm and hold it across the chest.	4 minutes	Preferable for children 1 year and older.
By mouth	Oral thermometer (has straight shaft)	1½-2 minutes	Usually for children 5 years and older.

NOTE: Be sure to tell your doctor which method you used to take your child's temperature.

TAKING BABY'S TEMPERATURE RECTALLY

1. Shake mercury down to at least 97°.

2. Coat the bulb of thermometer with petroleum jelly.

3. Lie your baby on his stomach and on your lap.

4. Carefully and gently insert thermometer about an inch into the rectum.

5. Grip buttocks firmly with your whole hand while holding thermometer lightly between two fingers.

6. Wait one minute and pull out slowly.

7. Read temperature. CALL YOUR DOCTOR if temperature is 101° or higher.

8. Wash thermometer with soap and warm water.

STUFFED UP NOSES

It's so sad when your baby can't breathe well because of a stuffed up nose. Our doctor says you can make your own nose drops with a mild salt and water solution. It works well. Ask your doctor for specific instructions.

Authors
Omaha, Nebraska

When my baby has a cold and stuffed up nose, we put a pillow underneath his mattress to elevate his head. You can also elevate one end of the mattress by putting a large book or blanket underneath. The slanted bed really helps the little one breathe easier.

Mitzi Worley
Omaha, Nebraska

SIDS - SUDDEN INFANT DEATH SYNDROME

Each year, between 6,000 and 10,000 infants die from SIDS. The cause is still unknown. There are two national groups for help:

National Sudden Infant
Death Syndrome Foundation
310 S. Michigan Avenue
Chicago, Illinois 60604

International Guild for Infant Survival
7501 Liberty Road
Baltimore, Maryland 21207

TUMMY ACHE

If your baby seems fretful with a tummy ache, take a warm water bottle, wrap a thin baby blanket over it, and tuck the bottle under the sheet in the crib. The warmth is comforting.

Lois Mahowald
Omaha, Nebraska

EARACHE

When your baby wakes up with an earache, it helps to rock him in an upright position with the sore ear pressed against Mom or to put a blanket against the ear to keep cool air out and heat in.

Lois Mahowald
Omaha, Nebraska

ORGANIZE MEDICINES

I keep all of my children's medicines, thermometers, nose drops, etc. in separate shoe boxes high in the closet. I label each item with the child's name, date purchased, illness treated, and dosage for that child's age. This is especially important for over-the-counter medications that do not always include this information on the prescription label.

Sharon Sigel
Marietta, Georgia

I never could remember what my doctor said to do when my daughter had certain ailments. I'd forget what things to do when she had a cold, or what foods to avoid when she had diarrhea. So I bought a notebook and recorded all of her ailments, how old she was at the time, and the directions given by her doctor. Now I simply refer to my notebook.

Authors
Omaha, Nebraska

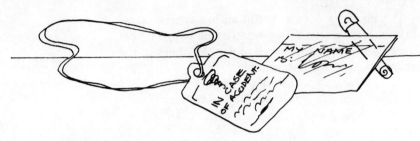

DOG TAGS

If your children have allergies or an illness such as epilepsy or diabetes, be sure they wear "dog tags" with their name, birthdate, blood type, and problem on them. This could be very important information in case of an accident.

Authors
Omaha, Nebraska

CONSENT FORM

Some hospital emergency rooms will not treat a child if the parents cannot be reached to give consent. You can avoid such a situation by giving your regular baby sitters a signed permission sheet stating your approval for the hospital to act, should an emergency arise. Once I was babysitting a 2-year-old who badly cut his finger. If I had not had such a consent form from the mother, the hospital would not have treated the cut.

Mary Kay Miles
Omaha, Nebraska

IMMUNIZATION

Every child should be immunized against the following diseases by the time he is two years old:

1. Polio
2. Diphtheria
3. Tetanus
4. Pertussis (Whooping Cough)
5. Measles
6. Rubella (German Measles)
7. Mumps

HEARING LOSS

Is your baby hard of hearing? Probably not, if he does the following:

Newborn: Should startle and blink to a clap. When called, infant should turn to you. Loud noises disturb him.

1-month-old: Jerks at a loud noise. Very aware of Mom's voice.

2-month-old: Enjoys toys that are musical.

3-month-old: Should stop moving or crying when you call him. Babbles when alone.

4-5 month-old: Baby will turn towards rattle, or some other similar noise.

9-month-old: When you stand behind him and call his name, he should turn.

If you think your baby or child is having some difficulty with his hearing, you should take him to your pediatrician and have him evaluated. It's better to identify a hearing loss early, so something can be done about it.

For more information on hearing loss, write to:

New York League for the Hard of Hearing
71 West 23rd Street
New York, New York 10010

or send a stamped, self-addressed envelope to:

My Child Can't Hear
Lexington School for the Deaf
30th Ave. and 75th Street
Jackson Heights, New York 11370

EYE PROBLEMS

Watch for these signs of possible eye trouble. Contact your doctor if your child:

1. Rubs his eyes constantly.

2. Has watery or inflamed eyes.

3. Squints a lot.

4. Looks at things out of the sides of his eyes.

5. Closes one eye continuously.

6. Has crossed eyes that stay crossed for long periods.

7. Always sits right in front of the television.

8. Holds books up close to see them.

9. Complains that his eyes hurt or bother him.

For a pamphlet on eye trouble, send a stamped, self-addressed envelope to:

Signs of Possible Eye Trouble
National Soc. to Prevent Blindness
79 Madison Avenue
New York, New York 10016

IN BED

Whenever Ben is sick and in bed, I try to make his time as cheerful as possible. For mealtime, I use bright paper cups and plates, and a straw. There are also less germs this way. I also bring out a new coloring book or wrapped toy saved for such a time.

Authors
Omaha, Nebraska

TELL YOUR DOCTOR

My child had an accident and was treated by a doctor other than our pediatrician. I assumed that this doctor would tell our doctor. I was wrong. Be sure you call your doctor to tell him of your child's injury.

Authors
Omaha, Nebraska

More Than One??

Adding other children to your family can create a Catch-22 dilemma. If your first baby is about 6 months old and has started to respond to you with smiles, hugs, and coos, then a second little "cuddle-bug" might seem like a wonderful addition to your family. However, eventually that adorable 6-month-old will grow into a rambunctious toddler. He will discover that hands can perform wonderful tricks like scattering toys, spilling milk, and throwing food. As for legs, they come in handy for making a quick get-away from the scene of the crime. You suddenly realize that your former precious little Mr. Innocence has turned into a wild man. He rushes from emptying drawers to hiding all of Daddy's shoes. By the end of the day, Mom's supply of patience and energy has been completely drained.

Just take a deep breath and summon up all the excitement and anticipation you felt with your last pregnancy and browse through these suggestions. They'll help you prepare your older children for the new baby's arrival and will suggest ways to keep the good feelings going after the homecoming of #2, #3, or whatever! Also take solace from the many mothers of twins who sent in suggestions. They are living proof that you can and will survive. We have provided many of their hints to make sure you will!

Preparing... 131

Mommy in the Hospital. 134

Baby's Arrival. 135

Dealing with Jealousy. 138

Twins: Daily Care 141

      Nursing. 143

      Using Your Equipment. 145

      Some Thoughts... 146

Preparing...

EASING THE ADJUSTMENT

These ideas helped to ease my 4-year-old's adjustment to a new baby. Besides reading her a children's book on pregnancy, we had her go with us to the obstetrician for some of the pre-natal visits to listen to the baby's heartbeat.

We often discussed what babies can and can't do and we observed them while we were out. We showed her photos of her birth in the hospital and of her as a newborn.

Susan F. Zalkin
Denver, Colorado

BABY EXPOSURE

When I was pregnant with my second child, I'd invite a mother over who had a new baby to see how my oldest child would act. I think this helped my 3-year-old understand what a tiny baby is like and she wasn't so surprised when her brother came home.

Authors
Omaha, Nebraska

EXCHANGE OF GIFTS

Before the baby is born, buy some gifts to exchange between the new baby and the siblings. This may help foster positive feelings. The older children can help wrap the presents.

Also, siblings can be included in selecting names for the baby.

Marsha Halpert
Albany, New York

RECOMMENDED BOOKS DURING PREGNANCY

- *A Child is Born* by Lennart Nilsson (Delacorte)
- *The First Nine Months of Life* by Geraldine Lux Flanagan (Simon & Schuster)
- *Our Bodies, Ourselves* by the Boston Women's Health Collective (Simon & Schuster)
- *Pregnancy & Childbirth* by Tracy Hotchner (Avon)
- *Successful Pregnancy* by Gary & Steve Null and Staff of The Nutrition Institute of America (Pyramid Books)

TALK TO YOUR CHILD

When your second child is due, tell the older child
that the new baby isn't going to be much fun right
away. Tell him that the baby will sleep a lot and will
take much of your time. Talk over in advance about
the jealous feelings the older child may experience.
Encourage the child to express all of his feelings.

Kathy Koch
Albany, New York

MAKE CHILD FEEL IMPORTANT

We tried to make our daughter feel like she was
partaking in having the baby. We tried to make her
feel important, stressing that *she* was going to be
the big sister, *she* would get to push the baby in the
stroller, *she* would get to help bathe the baby, etc.
We made her feel proud to be a big girl who can do
so many things while the baby will be very small and
won't be able to do all of the things she can do.

Authors
Omaha, Nebraska

NO BIG CHANGES

Don't make any radical changes for the first child
right at the time of the second's arrival. If #1 is going to be toilet trained before #2 comes, then make
it several months before or let it go until a couple
months after #2 arrives. Do the same with weaning.
Don't let your first child feel like he has been displaced by the second child.

Diana Hill
Azusa, California

MAKE A BOOK

To help prepare your child for Mom's eventual trip
to the hospital, try this idea. Draw and write a simple book with stick figures representing the child and
his family. Show what will happen when the baby
is born to his mom, dad, and to him. It will be a good
book to read to him before and after the baby is born.

Francie Aron
Mt. View, California

SHARING A BEDROOM

When your new baby is going to move in with your
older child, include the older sibling in the rearrang-
ing of his bedroom. Have him pick where he and the
baby are going to sleep. He can decorate the wall
next to the baby's crib. Allow them each some
privacy. Buy a partition and set it up in the middle
of the room.

Authors
Omaha, Nebraska

A BEEPER FOR EXPECTANT DADDIES

During my last few weeks of pregnancy, a friend
came up with a perfect gift for the daddy-to-be. He
loaned my husband a beeper so I could reach him instantly anywhere. The device saved my husband a
lot of worrying that he would miss the big event.

Authors
Omaha, Nebraska

BOOKS ABOUT THE COMING OF A NEW BABY (Here are some books
to read to your preschoolers before they have a new brother or sister.
They're good to read after the baby is born, also.)

- *That New Baby!* by Patricia Relf (Golden Press, Western)
- *The Berenstain Bears' New Baby* by Stan & Jan Berenstain
  (Random House)
- *The New Baby* by Ruth & Harold Shane (Golden Press, Western)
- *When The New Baby Comes, I'm Moving Out* by Martha
  Alexander (Dial Press)
- *Nobody Asked Me If I Wanted A Baby Sister* by Martha
  Alexander (Dial Press)
- *We Are Having A Baby* by Viki Holland (Charles Scribner &
  Sons)
- *Peggy's New Brother* by Eleanor Schick (Macmillan)
- *I Want A Brother Or Sister* by Astrid Lindgren (Harcourt, Brace
  Jovanovich)
- *How Babies Are Made* by Andrew C. Andry & Steven Schepp
  (Time-Life Books)
- *A Baby Sister For Frances* by Russell Hoban (Harper & Row)
- *Peter's Chair* by Ezra Jack Keats (Harper & Row)
- *We're Very Good Friends, My Brother And I* by P.K. Hallinan
  (Children's Press)

Mommy In The Hospital

MAKE EXPLANATIONS

When I went to the hospital, my husband told our
2-year-old where I was and what I was doing as often
as the child asked. I left him little notes, cards, and
letters with similar explanations. He found one by
his bed each morning when he woke up. He was
delighted!

Helen Cain
Omaha, Nebraska

MAKE A CHART

Put a chart of the days Mom will be gone on the
child's door, so he can cross out each day until Mom
returns. You can include a picture of Mom and the
child on the chart.

Francie Aron
Mt. View, California

HUSBAND STAYED AT HOME

My husband stayed at home with our 2-year-old
daughter, Marisa, while I was in the hospital. It
became a very special time for the both of them.
After the baby was born, I called home frequently
to talk to Marisa. We had previously purchased
several little gifts to her from the new baby. Each
day I'd call and tell her where to look for them. I
think between Daddy being home and my surprise
calls, Marisa really enjoyed that particular week.

Mary Jane DiChiacchio
Lansdowne, Pennsylvania

T-SHIRT FOR BIG SIS

To get Jen more excited about the new baby coming, I bought her a T-shirt with "JEN IS A BIG
SISTER" printed on it. It was the perfect thing for
her to wear to the hospital to visit Mom and Baby.

Authors
Omaha, Nebraska

Baby's Arrival

HUSBAND HOLDS BABY

At the hospital, my husband held the baby while I went down alone to the waiting room to get my 4-year-old to take her home. In other words, I didn't greet her for the first time holding the baby!

I also let our daughter open all of the baby's gifts.

Susan F. Zalkin
Denver, Colorado

When we took our new baby home, I let my husband hold the baby while coming into the house. That way I could hug my 5-year-old daughter and tell her how much I missed her. Then I explained how to hold, feed, and play with the baby.

Linda Larson
Troy, New York

GIFTS FOR SIBLINGS

Several months before the birth of your next child, collect an assortment of small, inexpensive gifts. Wrap them and keep them out of sight. Then when friends and relatives stop by to see the new baby and give the baby a present, you can grab a hidden gift so that the older sibling also will have something to open.

Marsha Becker Sandersen
Yakima, Washington

SPECIAL GIFTS FOR A NEW MOM AND BABY

TIME -   Offer to babysit to allow Mom a few hours of freedom. If she has older children, see if you can take them with you for part of a day so she has time to rest or be with the new baby. Offer your time to run some errands for her.

FOOD -   Make a meal for the new family or take over some baked goods or a fruit salad. Don't make a spicy meal if Mom is nursing.

GROCERY SHOPPING - Ask if you can pick up some items for Mom at the store. Call and get a list. Or just bring over what you think she needs.

DIAPER SERVICE - Paying for one or two weeks of a diaper service would make a great present! It will save a new Mom time and money.

SICK KIT - Pack a kit full of items that will help Baby get over any ailments. Include children's aspirin, a rectal thermometer, a nose syringe, gauze, diaper rash ointment, and anything else you can think of.*

HELPFUL VISITS - New moms get lots of visitors which may make good company but could put her behind with daily chores. When you visit, offer to help with something. Feed the baby, pick up toys, help with the laundry, play with the older children, take the baby out for a walk. Let Mom have a break!

BABY OR PARENT MAGAZINE SUBSCRIPTION

BOOKS ON CHILDCARE

BLENDER OR FOOD GRINDER

                                        *This hint is by Linda Larson
                                        Troy, New York

A BABY DOLL

When I brought home our baby, I also brought a
baby doll for her 3½-year-old sister. When Mommy
fed or bathed the baby, Big Sister fed or bathed her
new doll.

Julie Van Raalte
Holland, Michigan

PAPER DIAPERS

I planned to wash my baby's diapers, but I was
so exhausted the first few weeks at home that I
resorted to disposable diapers. As soon as I regain-
ed some energy, I started washing them.

Authors
Omaha, Nebraska

RESTORING PEACE

To make sure that my first month home with my
baby would be as calm as possible, I did the following two things. I took the phone off the hook when
I was busy with her. When we took naps, I not only
kept the phone off the hook, I also put a sign on the
door saying "Resting. Please do not disturb until
after 4:00 P.M. today. Thank you."

Authors
Omaha, Nebraska

Dealing With Jealousy

NOTHING LIKE GRANDMA

When your new baby comes, there's nothing like Grandma to help the older one adjust. My mom really helped our 3-year-old daughter conquer any feelings of jealousy when our baby arrived. She overloaded her with attention, which not only was good for my daughter but it helped me have time for the baby. Grandma didn't avoid the baby. She just moved slowly in showing him attention.

Authors
Omaha, Nebraska

TEACHER

One way to decrease the jealousy between my two children is to put my oldest into the role of teacher. "Jen, would you show your baby brother how to work his toy. He doesn't know how."

Authors
Omaha, Nebraska

LET HER HELP

I let my 3½-year-old feed my 10-month-old baby whenever she wants to, no matter how messy it gets. I feel this encourages sibling closeness as she feels like she is helping me and her brother. Occasionally, I let her choose the baby food he is to eat also.

Authors
Omaha, Nebraska

When Elisabeth's baby sister Tamar gets restless, I put her in a fold-up stroller and Big Sister wheels her through the rooms of the house. Both of them love this, especially Elisabeth. It's a chance for her to learn to push Baby Sister carefully and to help Mom.

Madeleine Soferr
Swampscott, Massachusetts

BACK TO BABYHOOD

When the baby arrived, our older girls became a little jealous. I asked them if they would like to be babies again and they replied yes! So for one day I treated them just like babies, including having each take a nap in the crib, taste the baby's warm formula, and play with tiny rattles. They soon started to tire of the baby treatment. What really did the trick was being told that they couldn't go to a movie with their dad and me, because they were babies, and therefore not old enough. They immediately gave up the game and became most content with being the big girls of the house.

Cookie Hoberman
Omaha, Nebraska

BIRTHDAY PRESENT FROM BABY

When the oldest child's birthday rolls around, buy a present that the new baby can give to him. This helps create good feelings.

Rodeane Green
Glendale, Arizona

PHOTOGRAPH

If your older child is in pre-school, let him take to school a photograph of the new arrival. When he shows the picture to his classmates, he will feel very proud.

Nancy Oberst
Omaha, Nebraska

CREATING POSITIVE FEELINGS

From the day the new baby comes home, tell your first child how much the baby loves him. "She sure loves you, Tommy" goes a long way. It makes the older child not only feel loved, but needed and special. It arouses friendly and caring feelings in the older child about the baby. The idea is so simple and yet effective.

Joanie Jacobson
Des Moines, Iowa

SPECIAL TIMES

When Baby naps in the morning, it gives me a chance to be alone with my 3-year-old daughter. This is a special time for us. We do whatever she wants for that 1-1½ hour period. I don't talk on the phone, or do other work at this time.

Authors
Omaha, Nebraska

Don't forget about the time you need to spend alone with your older child. My husband and I take Sara out to the store, museum, or visiting. We let her know that this is a very special time for us and for her.

Susan F. Zalkin
Denver, Colorado

SPECIAL WORDS

While talking to my new baby, I make his older sister feel included as well. For example, "Mark, there's your sister. She's building with blocks. She can do so many things." Or, "Jenny, your baby brother is looking for you," or "He sure missed you while you were gone." When talking to others I say, "Baby Mark likes to watch his sister the best." Saying these kinds of remarks really helps to foster good feelings between my two children.

Authors
Omaha, Nebraska

When the new baby, David, is sleeping I say just loud enough for my daughter to hear: "Now David, I can't play with you, I'm busy with Sara. We're going to play together." When I'm caring for David, I often call my 4-year-old by saying: "Sara, your baby wants you." Statements like these make Sara feel important and loved.

Susan F. Zalkin
Denver, Colorado

Twins: Daily Care

MAKING IT EASIER ON YOU

Try to get the babies on a schedule right from the very start. A chart will help you keep track of feeding, bathing, and napping schedules. Another way is to plan your trips up and down the stairs. You can eliminate some of your step climbing by having a diapering center on both floors.

Sheri Van Oosten
Omaha, Nebraska

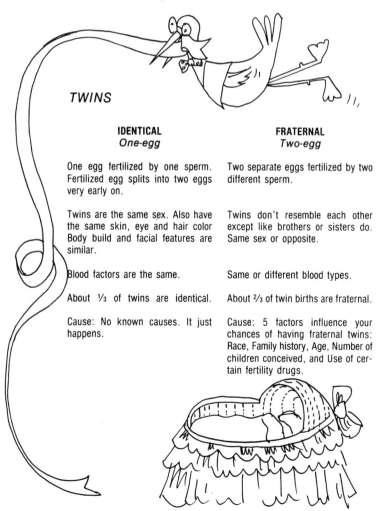

TWINS

IDENTICAL *One-egg*	FRATERNAL *Two-egg*
One egg fertilized by one sperm. Fertilized egg splits into two eggs very early on.	Two separate eggs fertilized by two different sperm.
Twins are the same sex. Also have the same skin, eye and hair color Body build and facial features are similar.	Twins don't resemble each other except like brothers or sisters do. Same sex or opposite.
Blood factors are the same.	Same or different blood types.
About ⅓ of twins are identical.	About ⅔ of twin births are fraternal.
Cause: No known causes. It just happens.	Cause: 5 factors influence your chances of having fraternal twins: Race, Family history, Age, Number of children conceived, and Use of certain fertility drugs.

BATHING TWINS

The best method for bathing twins is to give one a bath while the other one watches. Leave Baby A in his infant seat on the floor next to the tub while bathing and dressing Baby B, then vice-versa. Be sure to have all of the bath essentials assembled before you start to save time.

Sheri Van Oosten
Omaha, Nebraska

DIAPER SERVICE

Having a diaper service was a great time-saver for me. I don't know what I would have done without it!

Kathy Koch
Albany, New York

CRYING BABIES

If one baby is fretful but not crying hysterically, don't rush in and zip the baby out of the room. You'll find that your babies will adjust to each other's crying and won't be disturbed in the least.

Sheri Van Oosten
Omaha, Nebraska

SAME SCHEDULE

I am a mother of 1-year-old twin boys. I found that keeping them on the same schedule gave me more time. When one eats, so does the other. Nap time for one is also nap time for the other.

Diane Evans
Omaha, Nebraska

Nursing Twins

YOU CAN DO IT

Nursing twins is possible and can be enjoyable! It is necessary to eat a lot of good, nutritious food and drink a lot of liquid to keep up your energy and your milk supply. It is also important to switch sides with each feeding. If one nurses on the left side at the 12:00 feeding, switch her to the right side for the next feeding.

Authors
Omaha, Nebraska

I nursed my twins. I really enjoyed the experience but when I nursed one twin the other one would cry. I solved the problem by putting the crying infant in a rocking infant seat. Then I rocked it with my foot and could nurse the other baby in peace.

Toby Grubman
Philadelphia, Pennsylvania

SIMULTANEOUS NURSING

I found that nursing the twins at the same time gave me more time later to play with each of them. However, occasionally I let one stay up a little longer at night in order to give him a little extra individual attention.

Diane Evans
Omaha, Nebraska

Nursing twins simultaneously becomes easy with practice and even easier as they get older and can manipulate themselves into whatever position pleases them. While you are nursing you can read, sing, or talk to them, thus satisfying both babies in many beneficial ways.

Vicki DeLoach
Philadelphia, Pennsylvania

NO HASSLE

Breast-feeding twins is not only more nutritious than bottle-feeding, but we've found that it's easier. You don't have the hassle of wasting time washing and fixing bottles and nipples.

Susan M. Sperry
Hunter, Utah

FEEDING YOUR TWINS

* Buy formula and baby food by the case.

* Prepare formula to last 1½ days instead of 1 day.

* Omit a diaper change before each feeding, since most babies require a change after a feeding.

* A lifesaver for me: Make a schedule with Twin A and Twin B. Mark down what food each twin ate at what time. This keeps you well organized.

* Heat baby food in the jars with the lids off. This saves time and a dirty dish to clean.

Sheri Van Oosten
Omaha, Nebraska

RUBBER BAND ON BOTTLE

Keep baby bottles separated by using a wide rubber band around one of the baby's bottles. Now you can pick them apart at a glance. It's easy to remove and change the rubber bands when fixing new bottles. This is especially convenient when one baby has a cold and you don't want him to share his germs.

Karen Leonard
Omaha, Nebraska

BOTTLE FEEDERS

The use of infant bottle feeders was a real time saver for me in the morning for the twins' first cereal feeding. This is not recommended after 5 or 6 months as the infants need spoon feedings for their development.

Hazel Haralson
Gainsville, Georgia

MEALTIME MADNESS

When getting ready to feed my twin infants, I put both in infant seats on the kitchen table. I hold the bottle in one twin's mouth while feeding the other twin. Then I would switch so each got a turn at the food and formula. It's amazing how quickly mothers of twins learn to be ambidextrous! To prevent feeding one twin too much and the other too little, I counted bites! I also used the same spoon. Two spoons just made mealtime madness even more confusing!

Patty Nogg
Council Bluffs, Iowa

DINNER

Dinner time is a very chaotic time for us if I feed my 9-month-old twins and try to eat and serve dinner for everyone else at the same time. So now I feed the twins before Daddy gets home. Then Daddy, my 4-year-old and I can have a somewhat relaxing dinner while the twins watch from their playpen.

Marsha Itkin
Ottumwa, Iowa

Using Your Equipment

PLAYPEN

Introduce your twins to the playpen early. This will allow you more time to get things done and you will be encouraging the twins' friendship toward each other. They'll soon discover they have a playmate when confined to a relatively small space.

Sheri Van Oosten
Omaha, Nebraska

CRADLE SWING

A cradle on a swing that converts to a regular swing is indispensable for a mother of twins. The ones that wind up for sixty minutes are the best.

Beth Krewedl
Albuquerque, New Mexico

CARRIERS WITH ROCKERS
I am a mother of twin girls aged 19 months old.
I think the new carriers with rockers are a must for
any mother of twins. You can rock to sleep with your
foot the infant you just fed, while your arms are free
to feed the other.

Joanne Pratt
Swanee, Georgia

Some Thoughts On Twins...

FIRST YEAR THE HARDEST
Please tell other moms of twins that if they can
make it through the first year, which we all do, their
lives will be much easier. They will see that it has
all been worthwhile.

Hazel Haralson,
Gainesville, Georgia

LET THE HOUSE GO
Remind mothers to let the house go for the first
year at least. Also, twenty to thirty minutes spent
playing with the children in the morning and the
afternoon will make them more content to play by
themselves during the rest of the day.

Hazel Haralson
Gainesville, Georgia

When babies nap, forget about the housework and
spend the time for yourself! You deserve it and don't
feel guilty for it!

Sheri Van Oosten
Omaha, Nebraska

DID YOU KNOW that women between the ages of 35 and 39 are about three
times as likely to have twins as are women under 20 years of age?

SIBLINGS CAN HELP

I have twins and one child 14 months older. I also have children 5 and 8 years old. My husband supervises while the two older children feed the twins their 4 P.M. bottles. This allows me to get the evening meal prepared. I am free to cook and the older children feel included and important. I give time to my 14-month-old while the twins take their morning naps.

Hazel Haralson
Gainesville, Georgia

TWO SITTERS

When you have twins, having a sitter every once in a while is a necessity! However, I found out that I didn't trust just one teenage girl, especially when Andy and Cory were very little. So I decided to try two teenage sitters. It worked great! One was assigned to Andy, the other was assigned to Cory. It was worth the extra money for my peace of mind!

Marsha Itkin
Ottumwa, Iowa

INDIVIDUALITY

I believe mothers should encourage their twins to have individuality. I never refer to as "The Twins."

Kathy Koch
Albany, New York

HELPING HUSBAND

My husband and I shared a lot of the responsibilities when our twins were born. He was very helpful and got up for many of the middle-of-the-night feedings to allow me the extra sleep I needed. We shared the bathtime, also. We bathed them one at a time. While he was bathing one, I'd be undressing the other baby, etc.

Patty Nogg
Council Bluffs, Iowa

Find other mothers of twins by writing to:
National Organization of Mothers of Twins Clubs
5402 Amberwood Lane
Rockville, Maryland 20853

MAKE TIME FOR HUBBY

As a mother of 1-year-old twins, there is little time left for my husband and me to enjoy together. Breast-feeding the twins also cut down our time together since my husband couldn't help with feedings to speed up the routine. We solved the problem by getting our girls up early in the morning (5:00 - 6:00) and putting them to bed early in the evening (7:00 - 8:00). This way my husband and I have almost all evening with just each other.

Susan M. Sperry
Hunter, Utah

DON'T HOLD TWO

When I have a baby sitter for my twin babies, she is told to never pick them up at the same time. Even if both of them are crying, I instruct her to pick one up and comfort him. Then set him down before picking the other baby up.

Marsha Itkin
Ottumwa, Iowa

DRESSING TWINS

I like to dress my twin girls in identical outfits but in different colors. I buy my older daughter, who is not a twin, two of everything since I know my twins will get to wear them the next year.

Gayle Collins
Omaha, Nebraska

TOILET TRAINING TWINS

If you have twins, wait until they are 2 years old before starting toilet training. When they're older the job goes faster and is easier. Use two chairs and let them entertain each other while sitting there.

Hazel Haralson
Gainesville, Georgia

IMMUNIZATIONS

When it's time to have your twins immunized, let one twin get it one week and the other the following week. This way if they have a reaction, you won't have to care for two sick babies at once.

Susan M. Sperry
Hunter, Utah

Growing Up

When motherhood first hits you, it seems that your child's infancy will last forever. The drudgery of a constant routine beats you into a deep fatigue. Feeding after feeding comes at least every four hours around the clock. It seems that the diaper bag needs to be emptied again, each time you lift the lid. The days and nights blend together until you are convinced that you will be changing diapers and boiling bottles until you're 50. That little bundle of Jello who can only cry, eat, and sleep will never grow up. Your sleepless nights will hang on into eternity.

Then, just when you think it will never end, you notice that your little infant *is* growing up. At first there are subtle changes. She sleeps longer at night and is more alert during the day. Soon she smiles coyly at her best-friend "Ma-Ma" and gradually learns to call you by that name. She may not be living in a crib until college, after all!

These hints will help you cope with Baby's inevitable growth and development. Each new stage will demand your utmost patience and understanding. These ideas should help ease the transitions for both of you!

From Crib to Bed......................151

Toilet Training......................153

Shoes................................156

Little Helpers.......................158

Learning New Things..................161

More Thoughts... 163

From Crib To Bed

BOTH CRIB AND BED

I found that with my two older children, the transition from their sleeping in the crib to sleeping in the bed was made easier if it was a gradual move. If your child's room is large enough, have the bed and crib set up at the same time. Let the child start taking naps on the bed to get used to it. When the child is ready, take down the crib. When the transition was gradual, my kids made no fuss at all.

Diane Evans
Omaha, Nebraska

WHEN ANOTHER BABY IS COMING

We took down Maureen's crib a month before Machaela's arrival. Maureen went into a big bed and I put Machaela into a bassinet. By the time Machaela needed the crib, Maureen had forgotten.

Kate Cavanaugh
Washington, D.C.

MAKE IT SPECIAL

Moving my 2-year-old into a big bed came two months before our baby was born. We made the move seem very special for her. We picked out colorful and attractive sheets and pillowcases. We told her how proud we were that she was such a big girl to sleep in the bed. She felt very important!

Collen Brady
Rockford, Illinois

DO IT GRADUALLY

When transferring a toddler (Jason was 18 months old) from a crib to a twin bed, start by simply putting the twin mattress on the floor. If the child falls out at first, he can't get hurt or scared. About three months later, add the box springs. After another two months, add the frame. With this gradual method of getting the child used to the larger bed, there won't be the problem of him falling out.

Barb Wadleigh
Madison, Wisconsin

NO FALLING OUT

When my child started sleeping in a regular bed, I wanted to make sure he wouldn't fall out at night and hurt himself. I solved the problem by putting one side of the bed against the wall. The top had a headboard so that was no problem. On the third side I bought a bedrail. The fourth side was still open until I thought of lining a high toy chest against the foot of the bed. If you buy a toy chest made of wood, you can paint it to match the furniture. As the child grows, you can use it as a storage chest and add pillows to the top to create an extra seat for the room.

Rhonda Zwirn
Staten Island, New York

BUNK BEDS

When my 2-year-old daughter was switching from a crib to a bed, we bought a set of bunk beds. We put the extra bed downstairs, except for the mattress which we took off and slid underneath the bed she was going to sleep on. At night we pulled out the mattress. If by chance she should fall out at night, she would just land on the other "bed." We have 1-year-old twins so I know the bunk beds will come in handy.

Gayle Collins
Omaha, Nebraska

CHANGING ROOMS CAN BE FUN

Before our second child was born, we decided to move our 2-year-old from the nursery to a new bedroom. We knew the move could be traumatic, especially if she felt displaced by the new baby. We tried to avoid this problem by moving her three months before the baby was due. We also tried to make the new room look more familiar by bringing in her rocking chair, toy box, lamp and odds and ends from the old room.

Authors
Omaha, Nebraska

Toilet Training

DON'T PUSH

I started training my first child at 19 months of age. I was determined to train him, even though he wasn't ready. It became a very frustrating time for both of us. He wasn't trained until he was almost three. My thinking now is to wait until the child is interested. Don't force potty training just because you want to impress your in-laws or your friends. It will just backfire in the long run.

Authors
Omaha, Nebraska

STAR REWARD

Wait until the child can sleep through the night without wetting her pants before starting training. We had a star board to mark our daughter's progress. At first I insisted she put the stars in the right place, then I realized that was more for my benefit than for hers, so I just let her put the stars where she wanted to on the paper. It worked wonderfully. I also made potty training time our story time. The entire experience was enjoyable and rewarding for both of us.

Mary Jane DiChiacchio
Lansdowne, Pennsylvania

As a reward for potty training, try stars that stick on the hands or the forehand.

Kitsy Mavec
Mentor, Ohio

WAIT UNTIL THEY'RE READY

My theory about potty training, being a mother of two, is when your child is ready, he is ready, and no amount of forcing or bribing is going to make him be trained any earlier. Just play it cool, don't worry about it and he'll be trained sooner than you think. Sometimes I feel that the mothers who make the biggest fuss over potty training are the ones whose kids take the longest to train.

Authors
Omaha, Nebraska

MAKE IT EASY

When a child reaches toilet training age, dress him in pants with elastic waists. This facilitates his interest in using the toilet, since it is easier for him to pull down his pants himself. Avoid clothes with zippers, flies, and bib overalls. A child really feels like a big kid when he can go to the bathroom all by himself without help from an adult.

Betty Joyce
St. Paul, Minnesota

USE A TIMER

I could never remember when I had last put my daughter on her potty until I started using a timer. I'd set it every fifteen minutes. That way I could get involved in something without constantly clock-watching. This method really saves on accidents. It doesn't take long for the child to get the hang of things and Mom will start to learn the child's schedule. Then you can lengthen the intervals to twenty minutes, thirty minutes, and so on.

Diana Hill
Azusa, California

NEW UNDERWEAR

One way to inspire your child to be potty trained is to buy some new underwear that he'll want to wear. Underwear with cars or other objects on them, or colorful Underoos (Spiderman, Superman, etc.) might make your child want to keep his pants dry!

Cheryl Foral
Omaha, Nebraska

POTTY IN BEDROOM

We have only one bathroom in our house. It's inconvenient to keep Elisabeth's potty there, so I put the potty in her room. I have a small plastic container next to the potty where I always have some toilet paper. This works well for us.

Madeleine Soferr
Swampscott, Massachusetts

POTTY TIME

When my little one was about 2 years old, she used to "go" on her potty seat, but with no regularity. Gradually, I would schedule a time each day when it was "potty time." After breakfast, before naptime, and before bedtime. These were the times when she was to sit on the potty. These times became habit to her and kind of a game, and by 2½ she was trained.

Authors
Omaha, Nebraska

HELPFUL POTTY TRAINING BOOKS

Toilet Learning: Picture Book Technique For Children And Parents by Alison Mack (Little, Brown)

Toilet Training In Less Than A Day by Nathan Azrin and Richard Foxx (Simon & Schuster)

for children: *No More Diapers* by Joae Graham Brooks, M.D. (Delacorte)

PUT HIM ON BACKWARDS
The big toilet seat scared my son, so we discovered that if we put him on backwards he felt more secure. He could hold onto the lid and not be afraid of falling off the toilet or falling through the seat.

> *Kathy Becker*
> *Rochelle, Illinois*

Shoes

CLEAN SHOES
Trying to keep children's white shoes white is a near impossible task. Shoe polishes never really cover all of the scuffs. The polish also comes off easily on your clothes when you pick up your toddler.

I have found that it is just as easy to use a shoe polish remover and white shoe spray as it is to apply twenty coats of white polish.

> *Sharon Sigel*
> *Marietta, Georgia*

After cleaning Baby's shoes, take a raw peeled potato and rub it over the surface of the leather before polishing. The potato makes the shoe surface more porous so the polish is absorbed and doesn't come off as easily.

> *Susie Hokanson*
> *Omaha, Nebraska*

DID YOU KNOW that it is not a good idea to give younger sister or brother hand-me-down shoes? Each foot is different and needs a separate fitting. Wearing a sibling's shoes could be harmful.

SHOE LACES

Don't forget to whiten the shoe laces. Dirty laces are a dead giveaway. An easy way to clean the laces is to saturate them with a prewash spray and put them in the washer with the regular load.

Sharon Sigel
Marietta, Georgia

WHEN TO CHECK YOUR CHILD'S SHOES

CHILD'S AGE   CHECK ABOUT EVERY

* 8 months-1½ years.................. 1½-2 months

  1½-2 years........................ 2½-3 months

  2-5 years......................... 2-4 months

* You may or may not put your child in shoes at 8 months of age.

If the shoe *does not* fit:

* His feet have red spots. (Shoes may be too snug.)
* His toes have pink spots. (Shoes may be too short.)
* He has blisters and calluses.
* He constantly takes off his shoes.
* Don't forget the socks! Be sure and buy the right size. They shouldn't be too tight or short. This could be very harmful to your child's foot.

SWEATBANDS

To keep a toddler's trousers from becoming untucked from inside his boots, put adult tennis arm sweatbands (the stretchy knitted kind) around the bottom of each pant leg.

Barbara R. Hussey
Albuquerque, New Mexico

Little Helpers

HOUSEHOLD HELP

We've found that the more involved our 4-year-old daughter is with household activities, the more cooperative she is. She dries unbreakable items after dinner which keeps her busy while I'm cleaning up. She loves to help clean the bathtub after a bath. She'll dust while I'm dusting, help clean the lint filter in the dryer, fold clothes, etc.

Susan F. Zalkin
Denver, Colorado

CLEANING

My child has been given his own mop, broom, and duster to help Mama while I clean. He wants to help and it keeps him busy as I do my housework.

Rhonda Blum
Meraux, Louisiana

LAUNDRY

Let your 2-year-old pull clothes out of the dryer and put them in the laundry basket. He'll also love to put towels in drawers.

Nancy Oberst
Omaha, Nebraska

RESPONSIBILITY IS FUN

We give Marisa all of the responsibility she wants and she loves it! At 3½, she makes her own bed, helps me make mine, and puts on her own clothes with my help. After the clothes are worn, she puts them in the hamper or on a hook in her closet. She helps me put clothes into the dryer and then folds them. She also takes the dishes out of the dishwasher with my assistance. To her, all these tasks are fun, but I don't press her to help if she doesn't feel like it.

Mary Jane DiChiacchio
Lansdowne, Pennsylvania

HELP WITH DISHES

To encourage our pre-schooler to help us clean up the dishes after meals without making it drudgery for her, my husband and I ask her, "What *one* item do you want to clear off the table?" This allows her to make a decision and help us at the same time. Usually, she brings more than one dish on her own.

Authors
Omaha, Nebraska

SELF-RELIANCE

When I was two months pregnant, I had surgery on my back and wasn't able to lift. At that time, I had three young children. I found that little children can be taught to crawl into beds, highchairs, and up and down steps. When the kids were two years old and older, one child would get on all fours in front of a water fountain and the other would stand on her back to get a drink. Children can become quite self-reliant if you are there in case they should need you.

Hazel Haralson
Gainesville, Georgia

WASHING FOOD

To help Mom prepare dinner, I let my 2-year-old wash some vegetables and fruit. For example, if we're having green beans, she washes each one individually, breaks them, and lies each very neatly on a paper towel. This makes her feel very helpful!

Authors
Omaha, Nebraska

BAKING

While baking, little ones can be a great help by mixing dry ingredients with only a little help from Mommy. Also, they can add dry ingredients a little at a time, so Mommy can keep the mixing going. Of course, a little may be spilled, but usually not enough to hurt the recipe.

Diana Hill
Azusa, California

On bread-baking day, I make lots of dough and my 3-year-old makes his own loaf. He loves to knead the dough and it comes out as edible as any adult could make. He's learning some fundamentals of cooking without knowing it!

Debbie Karplus
Champaign, Illinois

LITTLE COOK

My 3-year-old is able to: crack eggs and beat them; get orange juice out of a can and into the pitcher; make jello; peel the shell off of hard-boiled eggs; and make most of her own lunches by spreading peanut butter, cream cheese, sour cream, butter or mashed avocado on bread. Kids can do a lot if you let them.

Authors
Omaha, Nebraska

KITCHEN HELP

I let my 2-year-old help with the dishes and it amuses him for at least a half hour. I simply put a large plastic bib on him so he won't get wet and let him stand on a chair by the sink. He washes the plastic dishes.

Susan Trotter
Rockford, Illinois

COOKBOOKS TO USE WITH LITTLE ONES

Kids Are Natural Cooks by Parents Nursery School (Houghton Mifflin)

The Natural Snack Cookbook by Jill Pinkwater (Four Winds Press)

Learning New Things

WALKING

When your child is learning to walk, there will be literally lots of ups and downs. When my child took a rough fall, it would take a lot of comfort to quiet her crying. Most of the time, she was just scared, not hurt. I found that if I gave her something to do right after a fall, she would forget about crying. I would just tell her to brush off her hands or her knees and I would do it myself to show her how. It made a game out of minor accidents and kept her happy.

Deborah Levin-Brown
Miami Beach, Florida

STAIR GATE

When our toddler was learning to walk up and down steps, it was too difficult and dangerous for her to go up all of the steps at one time. So we put our stair gate four stairs up and let her practice going up and down the four steps.

Authors
Omaha, Nebraska

TRANSITIONS

We have found that when making any transition with our son (weaning from the bottle, changing from crib to bed, taking the pacifier away, or changing from diapers to underpants) the "cold turkey" method worked the best. Once you've made the decision, you can expect a few days of problems, but when you get through that, the child generally adjusts to the change beautifully.

Barb Wadleigh
Madison, Wisconsin

TYING SHOES

I tied knots at the end of my toddler's shoe laces so that he couldn't take the laces out.

Linda Vogel
Omaha, Nebraska

To help my toddlers learn how to tie, I tied two shoe laces to two cupboard door handles. The children can practice tying whenever they want.

Linda Reikert
Castleton, New York

LEFT OR RIGHT

This is for your young child who can put his shoes on, but doesn't know which one is the left and which one is the right shoe. Have him draw (or you do it) an "L" on the bottom of the left one and an "R" on the bottom of the right shoe.

Authors
Omaha, Nebraska

BUCKLING BELT

When Ben was learning to buckle his belt, he didn't know which hole to put it through. So I marked the hole with a little black dot right under it, using a marking pen.

Authors
Omaha, Nebraska

Closet Rod for your Child

For information on an adjustable closet rod that hangs down from your child's regular rod, write to:

Lee-Rowan
6301 Etzel Avenue
St. Louis, Missouri 63133

HANGING UP CLOTHES
I have a second lower clothes bar in the bedroom closets. My 18-month-old hangs up his clothes while I fold the rest.

Rhonda Blum
Meraux, Louisiana

MORE THOUGHTS...

DISCIPLINE
I discipline my child according to her attitude rather than by her behavior. Some of her actions are accidental while others are intentional. While some incidents stem from curiosity, others stem from rebellion and anger.

Also, when teaching your baby how to leave things on your table alone, put away your valuables and teach him with non-valuables. That way, if he does disobey, nothing of real value will be broken.

Inez Davis
Kansas City, Missouri

CONSISTENCY
Be consistent, whether it be with regard to bedtime or carrying out a threat. Also, never make a threat you can't carry out.

Mary Jane DiChiacchio
Lansdowne, Pennsylvania

GIVE THEM A CHOICE

We have five children, ages thirteen and under. Right now, the way I deal with problem situations is to give the child two alternatives, either of which is acceptable to me.

For example, it is lunch time and a child may not want to eat what I have in mind. The alternatives could be, "Do you want cheese or peanut butter and jelly?" Sometimes I ask my children if they want their sandwiches cut in triangles or rectangles.

Often a child who is just becoming verbal only wants to assert independence within limits. This method also works with older children. It gives a child practice in making decisions and seeing the consequences.

Rona Michelson
Eatontown, New Jersey

AN APPROACH TO LIFE

Some parents seem unaware that their babies and toddlers will become children and teenagers. They should remember that the patterns they establish now will carry over into their children's later years. My basic approach to my children is to make them feel that they are people of worth. I try to help them achieve their potentials. I respect each as an individual with their own preferences, interests, and abilities. However, I also make them understand that parents are individuals too, with needs and preferences and that sometimes there may be a conflict between their wishes and mine. In that case, we try to help each other. Sometimes I will give up what I want for my children and sometimes I will expect them to give up what they want for me. Most important, I make them understand that my love for them is unconditional always.

Rona Michelson
Eatontown, New Jersey

Miscellaneous

Can you imagine trying to write a job description for the position of motherhood? Just making a list of the skills required would be a never ending task because each day on the job demands previously unthought-of duties.

For instance, motherhood calls upon exotic skills, such as playing the role of an imaginary monster. A mom must also make tears disappear, ease the pain of a wound with just the tone of her voice, and draw giggles by going on a reckless tickling spree.

The job can be dangerous. Mothers must often jump in the middle of flying fists to referee a sibling battle. When the neighborhood bully, bat in hand, heads down her street, Mom becomes a bodyguard to anyone in need. Sometimes in the course of her role as leisure-time director, an alert mom must duck flying balls, blocks, and other airborne matter.

At times, it seems as though only intellectual giants should apply for the job. A mother must manage the household finances with the skill of an accountant. Being a doctor or a nurse is a never-ending position. And then there are the more mundane tasks to be performed, such as cleaning, cooking, and chauffeuring. Other unmentionable chores take Moms to places other people with queasy stomachs would not dare to go. If you have ever known a child with a runny nose or diarrhea, you know what we mean.

Due to the fact that mothers play so many roles, it became necessary to add this miscellaneous category. If you can't find it elsewhere, look here for help!

Finding Time for Yourself............167

Working: Finding a Baby Sitter........172

Returning to Work...................173

Time and Money Saving Ideas........176

Pets................................179

Playtime............................180

Birthday Parties....................186

Recommended Reading................190

Finding Time For Yourself

CO-OP BABYSITTING

We have a co-op babysitting agreement among our neighborhood mothers. Each neighbor is issued a certain amount of tickets. Each ticket is worth one-half hour of babysitting time. When a neighbor cares for my child, I give her the number of tickets equal to the time she babysits.

JoAnne Greene
St. Louis, Missouri

PLAY GROUP AND MORE

I recently organized a play group for my 10-month-old. There are five mothers and babies who get together one morning a week for a couple hours of play and conversation. This gives our children a chance to socialize with one another, play with new toys, and the mothers get to compare notes. We also do some co-operative babysitting when needed. How nice to know you can get your hair cut or go shopping for a couple of hours without worrying about Baby. He's already familiar with the sitter and her baby!

Myra Weller
Austin, Texas

Do you want to start your own play group? These books might help.

The Complete Book of Children's Play - Revised Edition by Robert M. Goldenson & Ruth E. Hartley (Thomas Y. Crowell Co.)

Child's Play: A Manual for Parents and Teachers - Games - Toys - Play Groups by Lynda Madaras (The Peace Press, Inc.)

The Little Kid's Craft Book by Marian Lariviere & Jackie Vermeer (Raplinger Publishing Co., Inc.)

The Play Group Book by Marie Winn & Mary Ann Porcher (Macmillan)

STUDENT NURSE

I have a student nurse come to my house two half-days a week while I am home. This gives me time to wash and set my hair, study, read, and sew, and I am still available for hugs and emergencies. During the children's naps, the student nurse does light housekeeping.

Ann Marie Williams
Philadelphia, Pennsylvania

HELP FROM A HIGH SCHOOL STUDENT

Call a high school in your area that offers a child development course and see if they will let a student come to help you as part of their "work-study" program.

Toby Grubman
Philadelphia, Pennsylvania

REST WHEN THE KIDS DO

I have learned a trick about the kid's nap times. I lay down in the afternoon when they do. After all, Mom, you need a rest too! Even if you have a list of errands a mile long, it's more important to rest when you get the chance. You can do a lot of your work with your kids while they are awake.

Debbie Karplus
Champaign, Illinois

As a mother of three children, all under the age of 4, I have found it very important to rest when the children take naps, even if it is only for twenty minutes. A relaxing cup of tea and a book suits me better than a quick nap, because I wake up too grouchy.

Jane Colmer
St. Joseph, Missouri

HANDWORK

Toddlers love to play in the tub during bathtime. Of course you have to be there to make sure nothing bad happens but mostly you just sit there. Why not try knitting or doing some needlepoint while you wait? This works great for me!

Anthea Mazer
Omaha, Nebraska

BATH FOR MOM

What do you do with a one-year-old when you want to take a bath? I put my daughter in her walker and place it next to the bathtub. I set some toys and books on it and I take a fairly peaceful bath while keeping a close watch on my baby.

Authors
Omaha, Nebraska

PLAYPEN HELPS

Put some of your child's favorite toys in her playpen and never take them out. That way if she wants to play with those toys she has to get in the playpen. As a result she will love to be in it. This is a great time for Mom to take a shower or bath.

Debby Shepherd
Birmingham, Alabama

I have two children, ages 3 and 1. When I need to cook or just be by myself for awhile, I put both of them in the playpen and they play nicely together. Sometimes they fall asleep in there.

Sally Lewis
Albuquerque, New Mexico

MOM'S TIME

I have two children under 4 years of age. I love
being their mommy, but I have found that I need at
least one hour a day to call my own: to read, nap or
do whatever I feel like doing. I get this hour in the
afternoon when they take their naps.

Authors
Omaha, Nebraska

Even though Jason does not take an afternoon
nap, he has a quiet time every day. He goes to his
room and is alone and plays for a short time. His abili-
ty to play by himself has improved because of this,
and it gives me a chance to rest.

Barb Wadleigh
Madison, Wisconsin

SHARE WITH HUSBAND

My husband and I take turns sleeping late on the
weekends and it feels fantastic to sleep until you
wake up on your own! We also take turns putting
the children to bed.

Mary Jane DiChiacchio
Lansdowne, Pennsylvania

DADDY SITS

I don't get out very much during the day, so one
night a week my husband babysits after dinner. This
way I have a few hours to shop and do errands on
my own. It's also a special time for closeness between
my husband and our children.

Authors
Omaha, Nebraska

TIME FOR THE TWO OF YOU

Time alone with your husband is very important
whether you have one child or five. Get a baby sitter, even if only for a few hours, and you and your
husband get out by yourselves! Your children will
grow up and leave you some day, but you and your
husband have a lifetime to spend together. Make
sure you don't neglect each other.

Susan Gioia
Carpinteria, California

With four children under the age of 6, my husband and I need to get out of the house once in awhile. We make a point to spend time together once a week, even if we only go for a walk or a shopping trip. Sometimes we go out to dinner or to a movie. We keep a certain freshness and romance in our marriage by leaving family responsibilities every now and then. Of course, good baby sitters are crucial, but the effort in finding them is well worth it.

Deborah Gans
Goleta, California

FIND OTHER MOTHERS
When you have held a job and are used to having adults around you, deciding to stay home with a baby can be a lonely and isolating experience. I always suggest to new mothers to find other mothers in their neighborhood with whom to have coffee and lunch, while the children play with each other. You can also take walks or go to parks together.

Carolyn Lyman
Potomac, Maryland

AFTER YOU FIND TIME FOR YOURSELF, TRY READING ANY OF THE FOLLOWING MAGAZINES:

American Baby Magazine
575 Lexington Avenue
New York, New York 10022

Baby Talk
185 Madison Avenue
New York, New York 10016

The Exceptional Parent Magazine
Statler Office Building, Room 708
20 Providence Street
Boston, Massachusetts 02116

Expecting
52 Vanderbilt Avenue
New York, New York 10022

GET SOME EXERCISE

I was very lonely after my first baby was born. I didn't get out much, so my husband encouraged me to join an exercise class. There were other new mothers in the class and we'd discuss our babies. It helped me both physically and mentally.

Authors
Omaha, Nebraska

Working: Finding A Baby Sitter

THE SEARCH

When I began thinking about going back to work, of course my major concern was to find a competent baby sitter. My first choice was a sitter who could come to our home, but this proved impossible. So instead, I found a woman near my home who had older children. This seemed to be better than a sitter who has another baby to care for. The older children need only minimal care, and they were in school part of the day. Thus the sitter was able to focus most of her attention on my baby.

Aveva Shukert
Omaha, Nebraska

We wanted a sitter to come to our house so we put an ad in the local newspaper. That didn't generate much response so we put up notices at a few churches, and we found a very nice lady who drove. The day before I went to work, I had her spend the day with us to learn our routine. That way, my son got to know her better also.

Erin Rinaker
Fremont, Nebraska

When I went back to work, our top priority was to find good child care for our daughter. We try to save money in other areas of our daily living, but for child care we wanted the best, no matter what the price.

Jan Vanderloo
Medford, Oregon

FAMILY IS BEST

If you plan to go back to work, someone in your family makes the best babysitter if it can be worked out. I went back to work part time and my mom and mother-in-law were happy to sit for my little girl two days a week. I know this is an ideal situation, but I've also heard of aunts, cousins and sisters who babysit on a routine basis.

Nancy Oberst
Omaha, Nebraska

CLOSE TO WORK

Since I work so far away from our house, I chose a reliable sitter who lives close to my job. This way I get more time to spend with my little boy, and we can make various stops on our way home to run errands.

Authors
Omaha, Nebraska

Returning To Work

TAKE A BREAK

If you plan on going back to work after your baby is born, I feel you should take at least two to three months off before returning. This is what I did, and the time off allowed me to become adjusted to having a baby around. I also had time to interview for a reliable babysitter without rushing. And I got a chance to *start* to get my body back into shape!

Jan Vanderloo
Medford, Oregon

FIRST DAYS BACK

The first days back to work were the worst for me. I tried very hard not to talk about my baby and instead asked questions to others about what they had been doing. This helped a little.

Jan Vanderloo
Medford, Oregon

PACK THE NIGHT BEFORE

Pack your car the night before you go to work with your baby's diaper bag, toys, and any other paraphernalia you might need, such as work materials. This saves time when you rush off to work the next morning.

Nancy Oberst
Omaha, Nebraska

WAIT TO DRESS

Don't put on your work clothes until you're ready to put the kids in the car. While you're getting everyone ready you should just wear your robe. This way you can avoid having to peel off oatmeal from your "dry-clean only" suit.

Nancy Oberst
Omaha, Nebraska

SHOWER BEFORE WORK

This hint helps me to have a clean baby and get to work in the morning on time. When my husband is showering, I give my 4-month-old baby to him, and he washes him by using the water spray, and I dry and dress him. This saves time in the morning and there is no mess to clean up. Both Baby and Dad enjoy it too!

Shirley Pitcher
Omaha, Nebraska

LEAVE FAST

If your toddler clings to you and cries when she has to leave the car and go into the sitter's house, don't prolong her exit. Make a clean and fast break. I have found that when I stay longer and try to reason with her, it only makes matters worse. It was tough to do at first, but it proved to be the best method for both of us.

Penny Endelman
Omaha, Nebraska

LEAVE A BAG

I leave a bag at my neighbor's house which contains diapers, powder, a bib, and a few toys. This comes in handy when I drop off my 15-month-old on my way to work. It keeps me from having to pack a bag for my toddler every time I go out and she feels more at ease having her familiar toys.

Sheila M. Correia
Stoughton, Massachusetts

BUY SECOND SETS

Before your baby is born, go to garage sales and buy a second set of baby equipment for the babysitter's home. It is too hard to drag an infant seat, walker, stroller, and other large items to the sitter's house everyday. Garage sales can provide you with an inexpensive second set of equipment.

Rodeane Green
Glendale, Arizona

BOOKS FOR MOMS WORKING OUTSIDE THE HOME

Who Cares For The Baby? Choices In Child Care by Beatrice Marden Glickman and Nesha Bass Springer (Schocken)

A Guide For Working Moms by Jean Curtis (Touchstone)

The Working Mother's Complete Handbook by Gloria Norris and JoAnn Miller (E.P. Dutton)

Working Mothers by Jean Curtis (Simon & Schuster)

Help: A Handbook For Working Mothers by Barbara Kaye Greenleaf, with Lewis A. Schaffer, M.D., Thomas Y. Crowell

SPECIAL TIME TOGETHER

Be sure to dedicate your days off to your child. Be organized and prepared so that he will look forward to those days. On my days off, I take my child out to lunch, just the two of us. He feels it is like a date. We discuss what else is planned for the day and what he has been doing in pre-school. He feels involved and important.

Linda Shrier
Omaha, Nebraska

Time And Money Saving Ideas

PLAN AHEAD

Juggling a career and motherhood allows me little time for shopping. So I've changed my shopping routine and now buy in quantity, whether it's at the grocery store or department store. For example, I make a list of birthday presents we'll need to buy over the next three months and I get them all at once. I also buy about twenty-five birthday and anniversary cards.

Authors
Omaha, Nebraska

BEFORE BABY COMES
When you find out you're pregnant, shop for maternity clothes in local thrift shops. The clothes will be inexpensive and usually in good condition.
Mothers from New London
New London, New Hampshire

SAVE COUPONS EARLY
Even though I didn't feed my baby solids right away, I started saving baby food coupons before he was born. I found the coupons in baby magazines and newspapers. By the time he started eating food, I had quite a collection!
Authors
Omaha, Nebraska

CRIB AND BED
We plan to have only one child, so we bought a crib that will convert into a youth bed when our son is older. We saved a lot of money this way.
Authors
Omaha, Nebraska

PILLOWCASE
I have found that a pillowcase makes an excellent sheet for a bassinet mattress. The mattress slides right in and any excess tucks in on the sides.
Jane Colmer
St. Joseph, Missouri

MAKE RECEIVING BLANKETS
Buy one or one and one-half yards of soft flannel and hem it. This makes a larger receiving blanket than the store-bought ones and it is softer as well.
Donna Hatfield
Monrovia, California

WASHCLOTHS
I cut up an old towel and made six washcloths to use on our baby. They're soft and didn't cost anything.
Janet M. Parent
East Hartford, Connecticut

ALTERING CLOTHES
When my last child outgrew her long pants, I trimmed them to make her some summer shorts. I did the same with her floor-length dresses. I cut and hemmed them so they would last another year.

Authors
Omaha, Nebraska

OUTGROWN DRESSES
When your little girl's dresses are too short to wear as dresses, let her wear them as cute little tops for pants. Even an outgrown sleeveless jumper looks darling over a long-sleeved shirt and a compatibly colored pair of slacks.

Inez Davis
Kansas City, Missouri

USE THE YELLOW PAGES
While taking a maternity leave from work, I spent many hours looking in the yellow pages of the phone book. With prices going up, everybody tries to get good quality merchandise at the lowest price and I'm no different. I marked down all discount stores and factory outlets. They often carry brand name clothes at a low price. Newspaper ads can steer you to garage sales where people often sell practically new infant wear very inexpensively.

Linda Larson
Troy, New York

SWAPPING
Our neighborhood saves money by having a once-a-month "trading fair." We swap clothes our children have outgrown and toys they are bored with. Everyone leaves thrilled with their "new" possessions.

Authors
Omaha, Nebraska

CHOOSING COLORS
With my first child, I always avoided pink or blue colored jackets, sweaters, and heavy coats. This way no matter what sex I had next, either could wear it.

Authors
Omaha, Nebraska

Pets

FISH AQUARIUM

My 2-year-old daughter has a fish aquarium in her room. My husband cut a piece of screen, folded the edges, and screwed it onto the top of the aquarium. Now she can shake the food into the aquarium, but not throw anything else in. Also, she is not tempted to touch the fish!

Gayle Collins
Omaha, Nebraska

DON'T NEGLECT YOUR PET

I treat my cat like a child. I allowed her to sniff my daughter when I brought her home. She also sat with me when I fed the baby and watched while I dressed her. I never neglect my pet because animals can get jealous and turn on the baby if you ignore them. Today my child and the cat are good friends!

Gail Furman
Springfield, Virginia

SOME DOGS THAT TEND TO BITE	SOME DOGS WITH NICE DISPOSITIONS
German Shepherd	Golden Retriever
Poodle	Dalmation
Fox Terrier	Beagle
Pekingese	Sheepdog
Doberman Pinscher	Labrador Retriever

IF YOUR CHILD IS BITTEN BY AN ANIMAL:

1. Immediately wash thoroughly with soap and water.

2. CALL YOUR DOCTOR at once.

3. Observe the animal for 2 weeks. If it remains well, it does not have rabies.

Playtime

AUTOMATIC SWING

When Anne was an infant, I hung a sheet of slightly crinkled foil on the side crossbar of her automatic swing. She loved looking at the changing colors, light, and shadows that were reflected as she moved back and forth next to it.

Karen Maizel
Lakewood, Ohio

When my twins were infants, the musical, mechanical swings were lifesavers! Babies can be propped up and kept very happy for long periods of time. The movement is soothing and it is nice for the child to be able to sit up and look around. They are great to use at dinner time when you are trying to prepare a meal for the rest of the family, or when you just need some quiet time to spend with another child.

Susan Gioia
Carpenteria, California

HOUSEHOLD TOYS

Give a child an expensive toy and what happens? He plays with it for 15 minutes until he is bored and then spends hours playing with the box it came in. Sound familiar? If so, here are some great "household toys" to amuse children. Bring them out when your kids voice that common complaint: "There is nothing to play with in my toy box."

* Playing cards
* Plastic containers and lids
* Pots and pans and lids
* Laundry baskets
* Measuring cups and spoons
* Empty plastic baby bottles
* Boxes - all sizes
* Sponges
* Washed out plastic bottles
* Paper cups

APPROPRIATE TOYS

Newborn- 1 year
* Rattles
* Squeak toys with non-removable noise makers
* Activity box
* Unbreakable teethers
* Large balls
* Mobiles & other colorful hanging toys
* Stuffed animals
* Pots & pans
* Nonbreakable cups
* Sturdy books

1 -2 years
* Push & pull toys
* Sturdy books
* Large blocks
* Jack-in-the-box
* Low rocking horse
* Dolls
* Toy telephone
* Snap-lock beads
* Stacking rings
* Large, easy wooden puzzles

2-3 years
* Riding toy (with pedals)
* Chalkboard (with dustless chalk)
* Large crayons
* Sturdy cars & wagons
* Hats
* Simple jigsaw puzzles
* Punching toy
* Tea set
* Play-size table and chairs
* Cobblers bench
* Big peg board
* Regular blocks & connecting blocks

3-4 years
* Big stringing beads
* Doll house
* Musical instruments
* Magnetic letters, numbers & pictures
* Finger or hand puppets
* Phonographs & tape recorders
* Tricycle
* Trains (non-electric)
* Lacing cards
* Blunt scissors
* Clay
* Simple board games
* Mom's clothes (for pretend dress-up)
* Paints & magic markers
* Shovel & pail

TOY SAFETY

Many toys are potentially dangerous for your child. Examine the toys carefully before you buy them. The toys you buy should:

1) be too large to be swallowed or inhaled by your child.
2) have no sharp edges.
3) *not* be made with lead or inexpensive brittle plastic.
4) be labeled ''Non Toxic.''
5) have no detachable parts that can be swallowed.
6) *not* have strings longer than 12 inches.
7) be appropriate to your child's age.

WHAT CAN YOU DO? Periodically, you can check your child's toys for damages. Then either fix them or throw them out. If you want to receive information about dangerous toys (or if you discover anything unsafe to report), write to:

Toy Safety Review Committee
Bureau of Product Safety
U.S. Food and Drug Administration
5401 W. Bard Ave.
Bethesda, Maryland 20016

or call toll free:

U.S. Consumer Product Safety Commission
800-638-8326
Maryland: 800-492-2937

open 24 hours a day

INDOOR TENT

My toddler can be amused for hours by playing in his indoor tent. I simply spread a blanket over a couple of chairs to make the tent. He loves it!

Susan Trotter
Rockford, Illinois

PLAY CORNER

My 3-year-old daughter has her own little corner. We call it "her school." I have a small rug there. She loads a shopping bag full of things to do and takes it to her special place.

Mrs. Shimon Soferr
Swampscott, Massachusetts

OLD PURSES

My children are all grown and I have two grand-children who come visiting often. What do you do with old purses or handbags? I fill them with small toys and keep them in a special place reserved for when the grandchildren arrive. They adore digging out these treasures. I change the contents from time to time so they won't become bored!

Jane Price
Vancouver, Washington

READING SPOT

When my little girl wants to read by herself she has her own "Reading Rug." It's a small rug in the corner of our family room. She either sits down on the carpet or sits in her chair on the carpet to read.

Authors
Omaha, Nebraska

PLAY-DOH-LIKE SUBSTANCE
Do you want to make Play-Doh yourself? Here is
a quick and easy recipe:
1 cup of flour
½ cup of salt
3 teaspoons cream of tartar
Stir in: 1 cup water with food coloring added and
          1 tablespoon oil
Stir constantly over medium fire until it forms a
soft ball. Knead periodically as it is cooling. Before
it is completely cool, place it in a plastic storage bag
and twist-tie it shut. This can be stored at room
temperature.
This recipe makes a beautifully fine-grained Play-
Doh type substance that is really a pleasure to work
with.

Diana Hill
Azusa, California

BREAD SCULPTURE
I am a grandmother who enjoys babysitting. I
have found the dough for bread sculpture to be the
best amusement for ages 3 and up. It surpasses Play-
Doh and the ingredients are found in the home at
a moment's notice. Here is the recipe:
Mix: 2 cups flour
            ½ cup salt
            ¾ cup water
Mix with hands. Turn on floured board. Knead five
minutes. With floured rolling pin, roll dough to ¼"
thickness. Cut out designs with cookie cutters or
mold as with clay. Bake at 325° for ½ to 2 hours,
depending on the size of the sculpture. It is finished
when completely dry and lightly browned. Let cool.
Paint with acrylic paints. Older children can put on
a glaze by using directions on a spray can. Finished
pieces are permanent and inedible. Small children
just like to mold and cut out with cutters.

Mrs. Abe Milofsky
Cincinnati, Ohio

PASTING

I collect miscellaneous household items for my 3-year-old to paste and make collages with. For example, she uses empty toilet rolls and pastes on them things like junk mail and stamps. She adores this activity and it keeps her very busy.

Mrs. Shimon Soferr
Swampscott, Massachusetts

Try this for a rainy day activity. Cut out pictures from magazines or catalogues. Glue the pictures on large pieces of paper. Wrapping paper is great for cutting and gluing. You can buy glue sticks in grocery and discount stores which eliminates the mess of real glue or paste.

Francie Aron
Mt. View, California

FINGER PAINTS

Use liquid starch and powdered Tempera for the older toddler to use as a finger medium on glossy white shelf paper.

Authors
Omaha, Nebraska

PAINTING

Save your roll-on deodorant bottles. Clean them out and put paints in them. Now you have no more messy finger paints!

Dawn Skinner
East Hartford, Connecticut

TAPE RECORDER

This fun activity for my daughter, 2½, was developed by accident. I had been taping her on a cassette recorder so we could save some of the adorable things she says. We taped her singing, counting, Mom and Dad putting her to bed, Grandma and Grandpa playing with her, we taped anything!

She absolutely loves to listen to this tape!

Authors
Omaha, Nebraska

Birthday Parties

CUTE INVITATION

Here's a unique invitation idea for a birthday party. Blow up a balloon, write your invitation on it with a colorful marker or pen, then let it dry. Finally, deflate the balloon and put it in an envelope. Mail one to each of your guests. The children invited will be thrilled to receive this invitation!

Lynne Elliott
Drexel Hill, Pennsylvania

DECORATING

My children always help decorate for birthday parties. They help me pick out the paper plates and cups, and tape up the streamers and balloons. I buy plain paper white tablecloth, and they color on it before we use it.

Authors
Omaha, Nebraska

VARY YOUR CAKE

For a younger child's birthday party, try a different type of cake: angel food, banana or carrot cake. These aren't as sweet as the typical birthday cake.

Authors
Omaha, Nebraska

CUPCAKES

Try serving cupcakes instead of a cake for your child's birthday party. The cupcakes are easier to serve and they are just the right size for kids to handle!

Sarah Gail Hytowitz
Norcross, Georgia

SMALL PARTY

I think that young children enjoy smaller birthday parties. It's hard to cut down the list without offending some mothers, so try to invite only the kids that are the same age.

Authors
Omaha, Nebraska

PICNIC PARTY

Jason's birthday is in the summer, so we can set up a picnic table and have the party in the back yard. Of course we hope for sunshine, but if it rains we still picnic, only in the basement or garage!

Beth Ginsburg
Omaha, Nebraska

COSTUME

My children have been to cute parties with live clowns, and once we saw Big Bird! Costumes can be rented and add to the thrill of any party! Daddy can have fun masquerading, too!

Authors
Omaha, Nebraska

USE A BABY SITTER

When giving a party for your children, ask for help from a baby sitter, especially one taking a child development class at school. She may have some great ideas for games. She can also help with the decorating, food preparation, and supervision.

Kathy Becker
Rochelle, Illinois

BUY SETS

Favors are sometimes hard to find. One time I bought big sets of things, such as some Play-Doh sets and split them into single items. The kids loved it.

Authors
Omaha, Nebraska

PHOTOGRAPH

For a cute favor at a small birthday party, take an instant picture of each youngster with the birthday child. The guest will have a great momento and it is also fun to show Daddy later on. If you don't have an instant camera, use any kind and include the picture in the thank you note you send out.

Authors
Omaha, Nebraska

CIGAR BOXES

Instead of using sacks to give out party favors, I buy each child a cigar box and fill it with little surprises. This way they get to use the cigar box later on to put things in.

Nancy Jacobson
Lincoln, Nebraska

HOMEMADE BIRTHDAY GIFT

Here is a great birthday gift for a pre-schooler. Make your own Play-Doh* in three or four different colors and give it as a present. Include some cookie cutters with the dough.

Diana Hill
Azusa, California

The recipe for a Play-Doh type material is on page 184.

FAMILIAR PRESENT

When taking a child to a birthday party, buy a gift that your child already has at home. This way he won't get upset when it's time to leave the present, because he knows there is one just like it at home.

Sarah Gail Hytowitz
Norcross, Georgia

WRAPPING PAPER

Here are two ways to avoid having to buy expensive wrapping paper for presents. I buy white tissue paper and have my children draw on it. Also, we use the colored comic section in the Sunday paper as cute wrapping paper for a child's birthday.

Authors
Omaha, Nebraska

RECOMMENDED READING:

Baby and Child Care by Benjamin I. Spock, M.D.
(Hawthorn Books)

Babyhood by Penelope Leach (Knopf)

*Baby Learning Through Baby Play: A Parent's Guide
for the First Two Years* by Ira J. Gordon (St. Martins)

Becoming Parents by Sandra Sohn Jaffe &
Jack Viertel (Atheneum)

Child Behavior by Frances Ilg, M.D. & Louise Bates Ames
(Harper & Row)

Child Health Encyclopedia by The Boston Children's Medical
Center & Richard I. Feinbloom, M.D. (Delacorte Press)

Everything You Need to Know About Babies by Linda
McDonald (Oakland Press)

How to Discipline with Love by Fitzhugh
Dodson, Ph. D. (Rawson)

How to Parent by Fitzhugh Dodson, Ph. D.
(New American Library)

Infants and Mothers: Differences in Development
by T. Berry Brazelton, M.D. (Delacorte Press)

Supertot by Jean Marzollo (Harper & Row)

Survival Handbook for Preschool Mothers by Helen
Wheeler Smith (Follett Publishing Co.)

The Father's Almanac by S. Adams Sullivan
(Doubleday & Co., Inc.)

The First Three Years of Life by Burton L. White, Ph. D.
(Prentice-Hall)

The First Twelve Months of Life edited by Frank Caplan
(Grosset & Dunlap)

The Mother's Almanac by Marguerite Kelly & Elia Parsons
(Doubleday & Co., Inc.)

What to Do When There's Nothing to Do by the Boston
Children's Medical Center (Dell)

Acknowledgements

We owe a very special thanks to these people who included our pamphlets when delivering diapers to their customers. They made it possible for us to reach mothers all across the country. Our first thanks goes to **Mark Goldstrom** of the American Diaper Service, Omaha, Nebraska, who made it possible for us to reach diaper services nationwide. Also, a special thank you to **Jack Shiffert**, National Institute of Infant Services, Philadelphia, Pennsylvania; **Jim Crouse**, General Diaper Service, Kansas City, Missouri; **Hannah La Rash**, Stork Diaper Service, Philadelphia, Pennsylvania; and **Marie O'Grady**, Stork Diaper Service, Oxnard, California for an extra effort made on our behalf.

Also:

Michael Benis
Dy-Dee Service
Phoenix, Arizona

Rick Corbetz
General Diaper Service
Denver, Colorado

Jim Corley
Infants Diaper Service
Birmingham, Alabama

Mr. Disanti
Dy-Dee Wash
Chicago, Illinois

Dan M. Edwards, Jr.
Lullaby Diaper Service
Atlanta, Georgia

Mike Howson
Dy-Dee Wash
Cleveland, Ohio

Scott Landrey
Dy-Dee Service
Boston, Massachusetts

Fraydelle Leekoff
Stork Diaper Service
Albany, New York

Todd Mainville
Dy-Dee Wash
Milwaukee, Wisconsin

Paul Maland
ABC Diaper Service
Phoenix, Arizona

Vick Michet
General Diaper Service
Windsor, Connecticut

Tim O'Neil
Dy-Dee Service
Pasadena, California

John Schlickman
Tydee Dydee Diaper Service
Rockford, Illinois

Doug Slatz
Crib Diaper Service
Minneapolis, Minnesota

Elaine Smith
Baby's Valet Diaper Service
Albuquerque, New Mexico

Adele Stark
Di-Dee Service
Pittsburgh, Pennsylvanis

Barbara Strong
Dy-Dee Service
of the Carolinas
Charlotte, North Carolina

Michael Varone
General Diaper Service
New Orleans, Louisiana

Yak Weinberg
Crib Diaper Service
Louisville, Kentucky

West End Diaper Service
Cleveland, Ohio

Blaine Wilcox
Imperial Diaper Service
Salt Lake City, Utah

We were astonished by the broad range of ideas that came with each mail delivery and delighted by the ingenuity of the tips. Our sincerest thanks to these people who contributed to this book!

Jeannine Adams
Barbara Arkin
Francie Aron
Charlene Baker
Eileen Baron
Kathy Becker
Mrs. Patricia A. Beebe
Susan J. Blair
Rhonda Blum
Jody Bomba
Sue Bradfield
Colleen Brady
Betsy Johnston Brewer
Deborah Levin-Brown
Helen Cain
Mari Calianno
Bonnie Campbell
Kate Cavanaugh
Mrs. Raymond Chenevert
Nora Chesire
Denise M. Clapham
Helen Cohen
Gayle Collins
Jane Colmer
Sheila M. Correia
Inez Davis
Vicki DeLoach
Mary Jane DiChiacchio
Sidney Diekmann
Mothers from New London
Lynne Ellicott
Penny Endelman
Diane Evans
Mrs. Virginia Fallon
Joan Feldman
Cheryl Foral
Gail Furman
Loraine Gallagher
Deborah Gans
Keren Garcia
Kathi Gillette
Beth Ginsburg
Lisa Ginsburgh
Susan Gioia
June Glazer
Mrs. Lee Goodspeed

Rodeane Green
JoAnne Greene
Toby Grubman
Ellyn A. Gunness
Margie Gutnik
Susan Guy
Lynda Halbridge
Marsha Halpert
Hazel Haralson
Donna Hatfield
Donna Hersch
Diana Hill
Cookie Hoberman
Susie Hokanson
Kathy Hungate
Barbara R. Hussey
Sarah Gail Hytowitz
Marsha Itkin
Joanie Jacobson
Nancy Jacobson
Connie Joanedis
Mrs. Richard Johnson
Linda Joseph
Betty Joyce
Debbie Karplus
Kathy Koch
Beth P. Krewedl
Mrs. LeRoy Ladnier
Linda Larson
Karen Leonard
Sally Lewis
Suzanne Luter
Pam Luiten
Carolyn Lyman
Lois L. Mahowald
Karen Maizel
Anthea Mazer
Kitsy Mavec
Rona Michelson
Mary Kay Miles
Mrs. Abe Milofsky
Dorothy Mohl
Laura Mott
Patty Nogg
Nancy Oberst
Susan Paley

Janet M. Parent
Carol Parsow
Mrs. William D. Pearson
Jan Peck
Shauna Petersen
Shirley Pitcher
Mrs. Joanne Pratt
Jane Price
Robbie Puritz
Linda Reikert
Erin Rinaker
Stefani C. Roth
Marsha Becker Sandersen
Deborah Sawyer
Cindi Schaub
Christian Seaton
Debbie Sessions
Debby Shepherd
Patty Sherman
Donna K. Short
Linda Shrier
Aveva Shukert
Sharon Sigel
Jennifer J. Sixt
Mrs. Dawn Skinner
Alice Smith
Mrs. Shimon Soferr
Therese Sorum
Susan M. Sperry
Nancy String
Susan Trotter
Julie Van Raalte
Sheri Van Oosten
Jan Vanderloo
Linda Vogel
Barb Wadleigh
Aida Waserstein
Myra Weller
Pam Wilczek
Ann Marie Williams
Ann Louise Wolf
Janis Woodward
Mitzi Worley
Susan F. Zalkin
Gail Zweigel
Rhonda Zwirn

And to the following people for their invaluable help:

Marcia Belmont
Terry Bernstein
Bob Cassman
Frederick Cassman
Mollene Cassman
Sandy Echt
Jan Fischer

Ruth Friedman
Debbie Fuhrman
Lynda Halbridge
Anki Javitch
David Javitch
Gwenn Lawson
Betty Marcus

Carol Parsow
Doris Rosinsky
Dianna Scherer
Phil Sokolof
Ruth Sokolof
Pat Welch

Index

Index

A

Accidents
  avoiding, 89-110
  indoors, 91-101
  outside, 102
  See *First Aid*
Apgar score, 8
Artificial respiration, 105, 107

B

Babies
  bathing, 19-22
  diapering, 26-33
  feeding, 43-50
  layette, 5-6
  newborn terms, 8-9
  nursing, 36-43
  sleeping, 6-15
  swaddling, 7
  weight gain, 47, 54
Babysitting
  co-op, 167
  finding, 172-173
  special help, 168, 188
Basement safety, 101, 108
Bathing, 18-25
  babies, 19-22
  1-4 year-olds, 23-25
  supplies, 19
  toys, 63
  washing hair, 24, 39
Bathroom safety, 96-97, 108
Bed
  crib, 5
  transition from crib, 151-153
Bedding, nursery, 5
Bedroom safety, 98-99, 108
Birthday parties, 186-189
Bleeding, first aid, 104
Books
  arrival of new baby, 133
  breastfeeding, 36
  cookbooks for children, 160
  doctor visits, 113
  first aid, 103
  general recommended reading, 190
  playgroups, 167
  pregnancy, 131
  toilet training, 156
  working mothers, 175
Bottle-feeding, 37, 42-43
Breastfeeding, *See Nursing*
Bumps, 103, 105
Burns, first aid, 106

C

Car
  safety, 78
  seats, 78, 82-83
  travel, 77-84
Chafing, 8
Changing tables, 32-33
Choking
  first aid, 107
  prevention, 55, 94
Circumcision, 8
Clothing
  infants, 6
  maternity, 177-178
  organizing, 68
  plastic pants, 30
  safety, 98-99
  shoes, 156-157
Colds, 114
Colostrum, 9
Constipation, 114
Cribs
  safety, 98-99
  See Bed
Croup, 114

D

Diapering, 26-33
  cloth diapers, 27-29
  diaper rash, 30
  diaper services, 28-29
  disposable diapers, 27-31
  laundering, 28, 31
  supplies, 28
Diarrhea, 115
Dining out with children,
  87-88
Discipline
  attitude, 163-164
  bedtime, 16-17
Doctor visits, 113-118, 128

E

Ear
  earache, 125
  infection, 115
Emergencies
  first aid, 103-110
  when to call doctor, 118,
    122
Episiotomy, 9
Eye problems, 128

F

Family growth
  new baby, 131-137
  sibling jealousy, 138-140
Family room safety, 101
Febrile convulsion, 122
Feeding, 35-58, 66-67
  babies, 36-43
  clean-up, 50-52
  fussy eaters, 55-58
  nutrition, 52-55
  toddlers, 43-58

Fevers, 122
Fire safety, 92
First aid, 103-110
  artificial respiration, 105
  bleeding, 104
  books, 103
  breathing, 105
  bumps, 103, 105
  burns, 106
  choking, 107
  medicines, 109
  poisoning, 107-109
  scrapes, 109
  shock, 110
  splinters, 110
  sprains, 110
Fontanels, 9
Foods
  baby food, 46-47
  finger foods, 50
  to avoid, 44
Forceps, 9
Formula, contents, 42
Fun activities, 183-186

G

Garage safety, 100-101, 108

H

Hair
  cutting, 25
  washing, 24, 39
Hearing loss, 127
Heimlich maneuver, 107
Household
  help, 167-172
  organization, 59-72
Housework, 64-65

I

Illness, 111-128
  caring for sick children,
    119-128
  common ailments, 114-115
  doctor visits, 113-118, 128
Immunization, 126
Impetigo, 9
Infant seats, 19, 21, 66

J

Jaundice, 9
Jealousy, 138-140

L

La Leche League, 36, 38
Lanugo, 9
Laryngitis, 114
Layette, 5
Learning new things, 161-163

M

Magazines, 171
Maternity clothes, 177-178
Medicine chest, 120-121
Medicines
  administering, 109, 119
  organizing, 121, 125
Mongolian spot, 9

N

Newborns, *See Babies*
Nipples, *See Bottle-feeding,
  Nursing*

Nursery
  decorating, 69-72
  furniture, 5, 69
Nursing, 36-41
  birth control, 40
  books, 36
  how to, 38-41
  supplies, 37
Nutrition, 52-55

O

Office visits, *See Doctor
  Visits*

P

Pets, 179
Plants, poisonous, 93
Play-doh recipe, 184
Play groups, 167, 171
Playtime, 180-186
Poisoning, first aid,
    107-108
Poisons, 108
Postpartum depression, 9
Pregnancy, recommended
    reading, 131, 171
Prickly heat, 115

R

Receiving blankets, 5-6, 10,
    177
Recommended reading, 190
Responsibility, teaching,
    158-160

S

Saving money and time,
  176-178
Shock, first aid, 110
Shoes, 156-157
Shopping hints, 85
Sleeping hints
  newborns, 6-9
  babies up to 3 months,
    10-15
  1-4 year-olds, 16-17
  problems, 15
  schedules, 8, 13
Splinters, first aid, 103, 110
Sprains, first aid, 110
Stair safety, 101
Sudden Infant Death Syn-
  drome, 124

T

Teeth
  first set, 116
  preventing decay, 45
Teething, 45
Temperature, how to take,
  123-124
Thrush, 115
Time for mother, 167-172
Toilet training, 153-156
Toys, 180-182
  household objects, 180
  organization of, 61-63, 86
  safety, 181-182
Traveling
  air, 76-77
  car, 77-84
  preparation, 74-75
Tummy ache, 125
Twins, 141-148
  nursing, 143-145

toilet training, 148

V

Vernix, 9
Visiting
  doctor, 113-118
  travel hints, 86-87
Vomiting, 122

W

Weight gain, babies, 47, 54
White mouth, 115
Working mothers, 172-176